Helping Children Become Successful Adults

A Planning Manual for Communities

by Arthur A. "Don" Mendonsa

Carl Vinson Institute of Government
The University of Georgia

Georgia Policy Council for Children and Families
 and The Family Connection

HELPING CHILDREN BECOME SUCCESSFUL ADULTS: A PLANNING MANUAL FOR COMMUNITIES

Editing: Emily Honigberg, Jayne Plymale

Design and production: Reid McCallister, Jessica Mendelson

Digital composition, layout: Lisa Carson

Word processing: Brenda Keen

Proofreading: Martha Elrod

Cartoons by V. Cullum Rogers

Library of Congress Cataloging-in-Publication Data

Mendonsa, Arthur A.
    Helping children become successful adults : a planning manual for communities / by Arthur A. "Don" Mendonsa.
        p.   cm.
    ISBN 0-89854-191-3
    1. Socially handicapped children—Services for—Georgia—Planning.   2. Socially handicapped youth—Services for—Georgia—Planning.   3. Problem families—Services for—Georgia—Planning.   4. Child welfare—Georgia—Planning.   I. Title.
HV742.G4M46   1998
362.7'09758—dc21   97-50392
                                                                                        CIP

Foreword

Communities in Georgia are concerned about children who are dropping out of school before graduation; failing in school or failing to progress in school at a satisfactory rate; becoming unwed teenage mothers; engaging in drug abuse and delinquency; and being abused and neglected by their parents. These conditions place children at risk to become adults who will be unemployed and unemployable, abusive and neglectful parents, engaged in criminal behavior, and subjected to poverty and poor health.

Georgia is establishing partnerships with communities to help children and adults avoid or overcome social and economic problems. To this end, the state has enacted the Georgia Policy Council for Children and Families Act and created The Family Connection initiative. The latter provides grants to communities, while the former encourages them to create partnership organizations to govern the development and implementation of plans. The Family Connection and the Policy Council both provide technical assistance to local collaborative initiatives.

This manual is intended as a training and reference resource that communities can use when addressing social problems and needs experienced by children and their families. The manual identifies and explains a step-by-step process for developing comprehensive, results-oriented plans. It also describes alternative governing structures that communities can adopt to oversee the preparation and implementation of these plans.

The publication of this manual is a collaborative effort by the Vinson Institute, the Family Connection, and the Policy Council. Author Don Mendonsa, a member of the Institute's staff, has worked with these organizations to enable communities to understand the pertinent issues in designing a governance structure to oversee the development and implementation of plans for children and their families. Mr. Mendonsa has served as Planning Director for the Gainesville–Hall County Georgia Planning Commission and for the Savannah–Chatham County Metropolitan Planning Commission. He also served as city manager of Savannah, Georgia, for 28 years, helping to organize and direct plan preparations to help children at risk in the Savannah–Chatham County community. Further, he was instrumental in the design and creation of the Savannah–

Chatham County Youth Futures Authority, which develops and oversees the implementation of plans.

The Institute's work with the Family Connection and the Policy Council is of special significance to us. It has made us a part of the efforts now underway to help children avoid and overcome conditions that can be barriers to successful adulthood. We are pleased to have been given this opportunity.

Henry M. Huckaby
Director

Contents

Preface

· ·

In 1991, Governor Zell Miller of Georgia requested the Departments of Children and Youth Services, Education, Human Resources, and Medical Assistance to develop a community-based, collaborative approach for strengthening the well-being of children and their families. The initiative developed by the four departments is named The Family Connection. The mission of The Family Connection is to encourage communities to create collaboratives that will be responsible for planning and implementing strategies to strengthen children and their families. Currently 71 counties in Georgia have Family Connection collaboratives. The goal is to have these collaboratives in all 159 Georgia counties by 1999.

In 1993, Governor Miller, by executive order, created Georgia's first Policy Council for Children and Families. The mission of this Council was to bring together the work of many separate initiatives and programs in the state whose efforts are directed to helping children. To carry out this mission, a ten-year strategic plan was developed that called for replacing the current fragmented and process-focused approach to serving children with one that is results-oriented, family-focused, inclusive, preventive, comprehensive, and community-driven.

To carry out this plan, legislation was enacted in 1995 that transitioned the Georgia Policy Council for Children and Families from one created by executive order to one created by legislation. This Council is responsible for adopting and overseeing the implementation of a comprehensive state plan that addresses the problems of Georgia's children and their families. One of the first actions taken by the Council was to adopt benchmarks for improving the well-being of Georgia's children and families. These benchmarks are presented in the Council's publication entitled *Aiming for Results: A Guide to Georgia's Benchmarks for Children and Families*. A listing of these benchmarks can be found in Appendix C of this manual.

In addition to creating the Georgia Policy Council, the 1995 legislation also called for each community to designate the organization that would serve as its Community Partnership collaborative. The community organization given this designation is the only organization that the Council will recognize as being responsible for developing and adopting a comprehensive plan for addressing the problems of children and their families in the community. Under the provisions of the 1995 legislation, an organization that will serve as a Community Partnership collaborative must first be designated as such by a joint resolution of the county and the largest municipality in the county, and then be approved by the Policy Council.

The type of local community planning needed to accomplish the missions of both the Family Connection collaboratives and the Community Partnership collaboratives in Georgia requires a much different approach than that currently underway. Rather than emphasizing process and the number of clients to be served, as is now the case, the focus must be on achieving measurable improvements in the well-being of children and their families. Further, rather than continuing the fragmented and categorical delivery of services to children and their families as now practiced, an integrated and collaborative system for delivering holistic and complementary services must be established.

This manual describes a step-by-step planning process that can be used to develop results-focused plans for helping children and their families. It is intended to serve as a guide to Family Connection collaboratives and Community Partnership collaboratives in their planning efforts and can be used

• as a text to help train the staff and members of Family Connection and Community Partnership collaboratives in Georgia in the planning process, and

• as a reference source for all community collaboratives undertaking planning efforts to improve the lives of children and their families.

My hope is that all who use this manual will find it helpful.

In writing this manual, I have had the good fortune to have a number of people from The Family Connection and the Georgia Policy Council for Children and Families review and comment on the drafts of this manual. I have also had the valuable editing services of Emily Honigberg and Jayne Plymale of the Publications Program at the Carl Vinson Institute of Government, University of Georgia. I am grateful to all of them.

AAM.

Introduction

Today, many children are dropping out of school, having babies as unmarried teenagers, committing crimes, and failing to develop the skills they need to obtain jobs. Children who are experiencing these conditions are faced with barriers that can prevent them from becoming successful adults. Communities face a daunting challenge—that of finding effective ways to help children avoid or overcome these barriers. Meeting this challenge calls for a planning process that (1) identifies the factors that can create these barriers and (2) designs protective strategies and interventions to remove or mitigate these factors.

Communities do not always have people with the kind of skills required to develop successful plans for helping children. However, these planning skills can be learned. This manual has been written as a resource that can be used to facilitate this learning. It is designed to introduce basic planning techniques to its users. To do this, the manual identifies, explains, and illustrates each step in the planning process. In presenting these steps, the manual provides examples to illustrate each of the concepts being presented.

But what is planning and what is a plan? Here the term *planning* means *a systematic process by which plans are developed to accomplish specified goals and objectives.* The term *plan* means *the decisions made through the planning process about the goals that will be pursued and the means that will be used to accomplish these goals.*

To illustrate these two concepts, we can look at the way we might plan a trip to attend a meeting in Atlanta. The meeting is scheduled for May 2, beginning at 9:00 a.m. We live in Someplace, Georgia, a community approximately 275 miles from Atlanta. Someplace has a commercial airline service that flies to Atlanta. Our goal is to attend the meeting. Given the place, time, and date of the meeting, our objective is to travel to and from the meeting at the lowest cost. To select the lowest cost means of traveling, we must calculate the cost of each of the transportation options.

The process of developing and evaluating travel cost information is a part of the planning process. Through this process, we will first calculate the cost of traveling by car. This calculation will include the cost per mile to travel by car, the cost of staying overnight in a hotel in Atlanta, and the cost of eight hours of productive time that will be lost while driving to and from Atlanta. Next, we will calculate the cost to travel by plane. This calculation will include the cost of airfare, the cost of transportation service from the airport to and from the meeting place, and the cost of four hours of productive time that will be lost while flying to and from Atlanta. After comparing the cost of the two travel options, we find that when we consider the cost of lost productive time, traveling by plane will be the least-cost way to travel. We then decide that the best way to accomplish the objective is to travel by plane. This decision is our plan.

The type of planning required to help children avoid or overcome the barriers that can prevent them from becoming successful adults is much more complex and difficult than the type of planning that is done for a trip. Planning for the well-being of children is a problem-solving process that requires analysis and research of complicated issues. Effective planning must begin by identifying the barriers to successful outcomes that children should avoid. Such planning must then identify the factors that can produce these barriers and design strategies that specifically target these factors. Unless this planning process is followed, efforts to help children avoid or overcome the barriers to successful outcomes will not succeed.

Unwed teenage motherhood is an example of a complex problem that cannot be solved unless the contributing factors are identified and addressed. Unwed teenage motherhood can be a condition that prevents teenage girls from becoming successful adults. Rather than systematically searching out the causes of this problem, an assumption is sometimes made that unwed teenage girls become mothers to obtain public assistance and that the solution is to deny unwed teen mothers public assistance. However, the evidence suggests that the causes of unwed teenage motherhood are much more complicated than this. Research findings and the experience of those who routinely work with this problem suggest that the factors that make teenage girls susceptible to becoming unwed teenage mothers include sexual abuse (which often begins in early childhood[1]), school failure, a mother who was an unwed teenage parent, siblings who are unwed teenage parents, and peers who are unwed teenage parents.

If these conditions make teenage girls vulnerable to becoming unwed teenage mothers, then strategies limited to withholding public assistance payments clearly will not be comprehensive enough to prevent the problem. Instead, strategies will be needed to help teenage girls avoid or overcome the factors in their lives that can make them vulnerable to becoming unwed teenage mothers.

---

1. See Judith S. Musick, *Young, Poor, and Pregnant: The Psychology of Teenage Motherhood* (New Haven: Yale University Press, 1993). Musick writes that a number of studies have found that more than 50 percent of unwed teenage mothers were abused as children and that the average age for the first abuse was 11.5 years. She also reports that most of the abusers were adult males: fathers, stepfathers, uncles, older brothers, cousins, and the boyfriends of the mothers of the girls. She points out that for these and other reasons, the current strategies to address the problem of teenage parenthood need to be restructured.

Planning strategies to protect children from barriers to successful adulthood, such as unwed teenage motherhood, is a multistep process. First, the goals for keeping children free of the barriers to successful adulthood must be established. Next, the number of children who are not free of the barriers defined by the goals must be determined. Then, the factors in the lives of children that place them at risk to experience the barriers must be identified, and the objectives for reducing the number of children who are experiencing the barriers must be established.

Finally, strategies for accomplishing the goals must be adopted. In addition to preventive and corrective planning, the process described in this manual emphasizes results and is based in part on the planning guidelines developed for the Model Cities program established by Congress in the late 1960s. These guidelines emphasized outcomes or results and called for a focus on the conditions that had to be changed to accomplish the results. The planning process presented here is also based on some of the concepts and principles of the Planning, Programming, and Budgeting System (PPBS) that was proposed as a policy decision tool during President Johnson's administration. In addition to highlighting results, PPBS also placed emphasis on making a cost-benefit analysis of each of the various alternatives for pursuing the desired results.

The emphasis on results and on preventive and corrective planning that is the basis for the process presented in this manual requires planners to look in new ways at the problems facing children and their families. It requires planners to make deliberate and thoughtful decisions about the conditions that children and their families need help in avoiding or overcoming. This emphasis also requires planners to search out the factors in the lives of children that can make them vulnerable to these conditions, and then develop strategies to address these factors.

This type of planning is hard work. The people who will be directing, guiding, and performing this planning must be committed and dedicated. They must understand that the problems facing children and their families are complex and will not be solved quickly and easily. They must be prepared to work long hours and many days and weeks to develop a plan. They must have the curiosity to ask probing questions about the problems facing children and the will to do the research and analysis needed to answer these questions. Finally, they must understand that the type of planning described in this manual cannot be done on a piecemeal, part-time basis.

This manual is presented as 10 chapters and includes a glossary and five appendices.

Chapter 1 presents the idea that not all children enjoy the protective supports and conditions they need to become responsible and productive adults. Instead, they experience success inhibiters that families and communities must learn to combat. Chapter 2 discusses the need for community collaboratives to help children who face these success inhibiters and identifies and describes the forms these collaboratives can take. Chapter 2 also discusses the need for collaboratives to adopt a vision to guide their work and their planning.

Chapters 3 through 9 provide practical guidance through the seven fundamental steps of the planning process: adopting goals, determining baseline conditions, identifying risk factors, establishing objectives, designing strategies, developing the annual budget, and designing a system to monitor the implementation and performance of the strategy plan.

Chapter 10 summarizes the planning process in a work plan outline, provides tips on staffing and technical assistance, and suggests that collaboratives can make a difference in the lives of children.

This manual includes a glossary of significant terms used, and five appendices. Appendix A is the type of chart that collaboratives can use when planning their tasks. Appendix B presents a format for preparing a plan, in addition to a comprehensive plan summary chart. Listed in Appendix C are the benchmarks adopted by the Georgia Policy Council for Children and Families. Five different types of forms for preparing a budget are included in Appendix D. Appendix E is a checklist to use in creating a legally empowered governing collaborative.

1 Helping Children Succeed

In a perfect world, all children will grow up to become successful, productive, and contributing adults. As successful adults, they will be self-supporting and free of public assistance. They will have the literacy and job skills that a labor force needs if a community is to compete effectively in the economy of the state and nation. They will have the skills and motivations to be effective, supportive, and nurturing parents. Finally, they will be law-abiding citizens who help to influence community policies in ways that further the social, physical, environmental, political, and economic well-being of their communities.

Most children will become successful adults. However, unless appropriate actions are taken to help them, some children will not. Instead, some of these children will become adults who will commit crimes and be sentenced to prison; some will be recidivists who spend much of their adult lives in prison; some will suffer from poor health; and some will live in poverty, only able to afford the cost of substandard or marginally standard housing. Some of these adults will abuse and neglect their own children, and some will be chronically underemployed, unemployed, or unemployable. By any standard, adults who have these characteristics cannot be classified as successful.

Unsuccessful adults can be found in every state and community. In Georgia, for example, the *Georgia County Guide* published in 1995 reported that in 1994 some 33,383 adults were in prison, and 130,757 were on probation. Also in 1994, according to the *Guide*, 318,906 adult-headed households were food stamp recipients. In 1993, according to the 1995

Guide, 60,488 adults were arrested for committing felony crimes, and 26,326 babies were born to unwed adult women. The poverty data suggest that most of these unwed women were living in poverty.[1]

A factor that contributes to the lack of success for some adults is low educational achievement. This seems to be a factor in Georgia. In 1990, according to the *County Guide*, 1,170,000 adults in the state, 25 years of age and older, had not completed high school.

Recognizing Success Inhibiters as Obstacles to Successful Adulthood

Unsuccessful adults do not come into the world as adults: they start life as newborns. The minds of these newborns are not fully developed. They are not born with values, skills, and motivations: these have to be learned. Along the way between infancy and adulthood, the children these newborns will become may experience barriers that reduce their chances of becoming successful adults: barriers such as poor childhood health, poverty, abuse and neglect, criminal delinquency, unwed teenage motherhood, school failure, and low literacy skills in reading, math, and language.

The barriers described here are called success inhibiters in this manual. *Success inhibiters* are *conditions experienced by children that can be*

---

1. *The Georgia County Guide,* 14th ed. (Athens, Ga.: The Cooperative Extension Service, University of Georgia, 1995).

Success inhibiters can be barriers to development.

barriers to the development of the values, skills, motivations, capacities, and personal relationships they need to become successful adults. These barriers have the following effects:

- They limit the capacity of children to acquire the literacy skills they will need to compete as adults for jobs.
- They reduce the capacity of children to acquire the behavior patterns, values, and attitudes they will need as adults to be contributing and supportive members of the community.
- They limit the capacity of children to become adults who will have socially healthy relationships with other members of the community.
- They limit the capacity of children to become adults who will be effective, caring, and supportive parents for their own children.

The following list gives examples of success inhibiters and some of the effects they can have on the children who experience them:

- *Low birthweight:* Infants born with low birthweights can experience such obstacles to well-being as physical and mental disabilities, behavior problems, and chronic poor health. Each of these conditions can be a

barrier to children becoming successful adults.

- *Abuse and neglect:* Children who are victims of abuse and neglect can be affected in several ways: They can grow up with little or no self-esteem. They can be vulnerable to school failure, drug abuse, and teenage parenthood. They may become violent teenagers who grow up to become violent adults. And they can become parents who abuse and neglect their own children.
- *Unwed teenage parenthood:* Pregnancy and parenthood can cause teenage girls to drop out of school before they have mastered the literacy skills they need to compete for jobs or to enter post-secondary education programs. Their inability to find employment can cause them to turn to public assistance for themselves and their children. Having had one child, some, while still teenagers, may have more children. Poor spacing between the repeat pregnancies of these teenagers can place the lives of their unborn children at risk. Another consequence of unwed teenage parenthood is the risk it places on the children. These children risk growing up in poverty, experiencing abuse and neglect, failing in school, becoming delinquent, and suffering from chronic illnesses and uncorrected but correctable handicaps.
- *School failure:* Children can be retained in the first, second, or third grades in school and never catch up with their age group. This can lead to their dropping out of school without developing the literacy skills they need to compete successfully in the adult world. Lack of success in the early grades of school can also be a factor in delinquent behavior and unwed teenage pregnancy and parenthood.
- *Criminal delinquency:* Children who have a record of violence and crime while young risk having a record of violence and crime as adults.

The 1996–97 edition of the *Georgia Kids Count Factbook* reports the proportion of children in Georgia who are experiencing some of these success inhibiters. In Georgia, according to the *Factbook*—

- 9 out of every 100 babies were born with low birthweights.
- 50 out of every 1,000 unwed teenage girls had babies. (Data from the Georgia Department of Human Resources indicate that approximately 30 percent of the births to unwed teenage girls were repeat births.)
- 6 out of every 100 youth between the ages of 10 and 17 were arrested for crimes.
- 37 out of 100 ninth-grade students did not complete high school on time.
- 15 out of every 1,000 children were victims of child abuse and neglect.[2]

In many Georgia communities, the proportion of children who are experiencing these conditions is higher, sometimes much higher, than it is for the state as a whole. As reported in the 1996–97 *Georgia Kids Count Factbook,* of the 16 counties in Georgia with populations of 80,000 or more,

- nine have higher rates than the state for babies born with low birthweights;
- seven have higher rates for child abuse and neglect; and
- thirteen have higher rates for births to teenage girls.

Many Georgia counties with fewer than 80,000 population also have higher rates than those for the state.

The relationship between the success inhibiters experienced by some children during their infancy and childhood and their subsequent lack of success as adults is not generally understood by the public. As a result, not enough attention and effort is given to protecting children from success inhibiters. Instead, many agencies and programs that serve children who are having problems seek to relieve the problems rather than prevent their first-time occurrence or prevent their recurrence. Providing temporary relief becomes the end to be achieved rather than the means to the end—achieving successful adulthood for children.

There is a fundamental difference between providing services to help recipients obtain relief from problems and providing services to help recipients overcome and avoid problems. When the purpose is to provide relief, then the recipients of these services can return again and again for help. The services they receive are not designed or intended to prevent a recurrence of the condition for which they are seeking help. Further, these services are not directed to preventing the conditions that create a need for relief.

When their purpose is to help recipients overcome and avoid problems, these services will place equal emphasis on providing relief, preventing first-time occurrence of problems, and preventing the recurrence of problems. This is a new way of doing business for most agencies and institutions serving children. However, if children with problems are to receive the help they need, this is the way agencies and institutions must operate. As they do business in this new way, agencies and institutions must recognize that children who are in danger of becoming unsuccessful adults can experience several success inhibiter problems simultaneously and that all must be addressed if successful adulthood is to be achieved. They also must recognize that some children who are not yet experiencing inhibiters are vulnerable to experiencing them and must be identified and helped.

---

2. Georgia Kids Count Project, *Georgia Kids Count Factbook* (Atlanta: Georgians for Children, 1996–97).

Encouraging Community Responsibility

▪ ▪ ▪ ▪ ▪ ▪ ▪ ▪ ▪ ▪ ▪ ▪ ▪ ▪ ▪ ▪ ▪ ▪ ▪ ▪

Communities must find ways to help their children become successful adults. If they do not, the quality of life of their citizens will continue to be blighted. It will be blighted by the fear of crime and by the costs of addressing problems created by a growing population of unsuccessful adults. A part of these costs will be a less productive workforce that results when a significant number of adults do not have the literacy and skills needed to be employable. A part will be the cost of public assistance, a part the cost of prisons, and a part the cost of publicly financed health care for unsuccessful adults and their children. Communities are already faced with these costs. Unless effective actions are taken to help children avoid or overcome the success inhibiters, new generations of unsuccessful adults will be created.

Protecting children from success inhibiters requires thoughtful and informed planning. This planning must develop effective strategies through which protective factors for children and their families can be created or strengthened and risk factors removed or mitigated. Such planning requires the commitment, participation, and collaboration of child-serving agencies and institutions, of local governments and the business community, of citizens and community leaders, and of the vulnerable populations and neighborhoods themselves.

Communities and their citizens must recognize that strategies to help children avoid success inhibiters can be effective only if they are based on a thorough analysis of the conditions in which children and their families live. They must understand that the successful implementation of strategies will not happen without the coordinated cooperation and participation of many different agencies and organizations; the support, influence, and actions of a broad-based community collaborative; and the confidence, respect, support, and active participation of children and their families.

In undertaking the planning effort, all stakeholders must recognize that quick solutions either to prevent or correct success inhibiters do not exist. They will learn that developing strategies takes time and that interventions can take several years to produce real reductions in the numbers and rates of children experiencing success inhibiters. They should not be discouraged. The results will benefit not only the children and their families but the community as a whole.

2 Creating a Governing Collaborative

Most people will agree that the outcome desired for children is that they will grow up to become successful adults. Most children will achieve this outcome. This will happen because these children will receive the protection, support, and assistance they need from their families, neighborhoods, schools, and community as they develop from infancy to adulthood. These successful children give credibility to the often quoted African proverb that "it takes an entire village to raise a child." For these children, the entire village is involved in their development.

These successful children are empowered children. They grow up in supportive neighborhoods and in protective and supportive families. The efforts of the families and neighborhoods of these children are complemented by timely responses to their needs from the community and from community agencies and institutions. These responses may be prompted in

Successful children grow up in supportive neighborhoods and families.

part by the power, influence, and social and economic position of their families and family friends.

Some children, however, are not empowered. They grow up in neighborhoods and families that are socially and economically disadvantaged. These families and neighborhoods do not have the power or influence to prompt responses on behalf of their children from the community or from community agencies and institutions. For these unempowered children, the "village" is not helping to raise a child.

Some unempowered children are succeeding without the benefit of a responsive community. They succeed because of protective factors at work in their family and religious lives, and because they have innate strengths that help them overcome or avoid the barriers to success.

However, some unempowered children are not succeeding. The protective factors they need are not readily available and are not provided by their families and neighborhoods, by neighborhood religious institutions, or by community agencies and institutions. To make the "village" work for them, these children need powerful and influential advocates who can prompt the village to respond to their needs. The challenge is to find such advocates and, when they are found, to bring them together in a structured and formal arrangement through which they can collectively and collaboratively work to make the village act. In this manual, such a structured and formal arrangement is called a *collaborative*.

A *collaborative* is defined as *an organization whose members collectively agree and commit themselves to the following*:

- To serve as advocates and activists for children.
- To adopt a common vision for successful outcomes for children.
- To adopt and agree on common goals for children.
- To adopt and agree on objectives for achieving these goals.
- To adopt and agree on strategies for achieving these objectives.
- To adopt and agree on annual work programs and budgets to implement the strategies.
- To ensure that participating agencies and institutions in the collaborative agree to carry out the components of the strategies assigned to them.
- To ensure that participating agencies and institutions in the collaborative agree to allocate or redirect funds to pay the costs of implementing the strategies assigned to them.
- To ensure that members of the collaborative are individually and collectively responsible for the performance and effectiveness of the strategies.
- To ensure that participating agencies and institutions coordinate interventions to serve children and their families.
- To minimize and eliminate duplication of efforts on the part of the collaborative members.
- To eliminate competition among agencies and institutions for funds and recognition.
- To ensure that participating agencies and institutions objectively, candidly, and completely report results of their interventions to help children and their families.

To function as collaboratives that meet these criteria, organizations must be more than informal gatherings of people, agencies, and institutions with common interests who come together occasionally to share information and concerns. Instead, these organizations must meet on a regular and formal basis. Their members must have the respect of the public and be able to influence the decisions affecting children that are made by policy makers and budget planners.

Organizations that do not meet these criteria will not be true collaboratives. Further, their members will not be listened to when they speak, and they will find that public and private support and funding for their plans and interventions will be difficult to obtain. In addition, these organizations will be unable to influence state and local elected officials, business leaders, and the policy makers for the agencies and institutions serving children and families. Finally, these organizations will be unable to attract the participation and support of individuals, groups, and organizations who are not yet a part of the efforts to help children and their families but who need to become a part of these efforts.

By comparison, causes such as saving endangered trees and historic structures will often fare better than children in distress. The reason for this is that advocates for trees and historic structures are usually politically powerful and influential while those who advocate for children often are not. Advocates for trees and historic structures use their power and influence to lobby actively and successfully for laws, initiatives, and funding to protect trees or historic structures from damage or destruction. Unfortunately, however, very few groups that are concerned about children have this kind of power and influence. As a consequence, their efforts to lobby to protect the well-being of children do not always succeed.

Creating Collaboratives to Be Effective Advocates for Children

Creating effective collaboratives can be difficult. Disagreements can arise concerning the method that will be used to create them, the powers they will have, the composition of their membership, how members will be appointed, and the purposes for which they will be created. All these issues must be addressed and resolved. How they are resolved will affect the ability of collaboratives to function effectively.

Types and Forms of Collaboratives

Collaboratives can be of two types: (1) those created as formal and structured organizations that have been granted legal powers, and (2) those created as formal or as informal organizations that have not been granted legal powers.

Collaboratives with Legal Powers

To obtain legal powers, collaboratives must be created under the authority of law. This can be done in two ways:

1. Collaboratives can be created as quasi-governmental organizations under the authority of state enabling legislation. Collaboratives created in this manner are formal organizations that can exist in perpetuity or until the legislation authorizing them is repealed. Under the authority of the enabling legislation, these collaboratives can be granted legal powers and authority. Further, the purposes of these collaboratives usually will be specified in the enabling legislation. In addition, this legislation usually will specify the composition of the membership, terms of office, and method by which members will be appointed and replaced. The legislation creating these collaboratives will usually specify the minimum frequency with which these collaboratives must meet, and the officers they will have and their terms of office.

Because they are quasi-governmental bodies, the revenues and expenses of these legislatively created collaboratives will be classified as public revenues and expenses. In addition, because of their quasi-governmental status these collaboratives will be accountable to the public, the organizations

Creating effective collaboratives can be difficult.

that appoint their members, and the organizations that fund their budgets.

Another feature of quasi-governmental collaboratives is that local governments can enter into multiyear contracts with them. Generally, local governments do not have the authority to do this with private, nonprofit organizations.

Unless a general enabling law has been enacted by the state that authorizes the creation of quasi-governmental collaboratives, communities seeking to create such collaboratives must obtain authorizing legislation from the state. Communities can do this through their local delegation to the state legislature.

2. Collaboratives can be created as private, nonprofit corporations under the authority of state statutes governing such incorporations. Unless modified by their Articles of Incorporation, the powers and governing structure of nonprofit corporations in the state are dictated by the provisions of the Georgia Nonprofit Corporation Code.[1] The bylaws adopted by the nonprofit corporation must be consistent with the authority granted in the Nonprofit Code and their Incorporation articles.

Private, nonprofit collaboratives are self-perpetuating and self-accountable organizations. They appoint their members and their replacements. Except when contracts with other parties dictate otherwise, these collaboratives are responsible and accountable only to their members.

Private, nonprofit corporations must periodically renew their registration with the state. In addition, all their revenues are private funds and cannot be used for grants that require matching with public funds. Finally, because they are private organizations, local governments usually do not have the authority to enter into multiyear contracts with them.

Collaboratives That Have No Legal Powers

Collaboratives can be created that have no legal powers. This can be done in two ways:

1. Collaboratives can be created as meet-and-confer groups. Meet-and-confer collaboratives are usually created to bring together agencies and/or individuals who have common interests and concerns about specific problems and issues. These collaboratives are informal groups that have no legal powers and no formal membership structure. Participation in the group is voluntary and at the will of the participants. To give some formality to their meetings, meet-and-confer collaboratives may designate one of their participants to serve as chairperson and may agree to meet on a regular basis. Although participants in these collaboratives may agree on "bylaws" for the group, these bylaws can do little more than establish rules of procedure for conducting meetings and for participating in the group.

Although they have no legal powers, meet-and-confer collaboratives can use the political power and influence of their members to develop, support, and promote the implementation of comprehensive community plans to address the problems faced by children and their families. In addition, many of the organizations that are a part of meet-and-confer groups have the legal power to enter into interagency agreements with one another. These agencies can voluntarily use these powers to carry out the provisions of the plan. However, meet-and-confer collaboratives have no legal way to contract with such agencies. Meet-and-con-

_____

1. OFFICIAL CODE OF GEORGIA ANNOTATED, Chapter 3 of Title 14.

fer collaboratives do not have the legal authority to receive grants, spend money, employ staff, or enter into contracts. These functions must be done for them by organizations that do have the authority to do these things, such as local governments, school systems, local divisions of the Georgia Department of Human Resources, incorporated community foundations, and incorporated private, nonprofit organizations. Because meet-and-confer collaboratives do not have the legal authority to enter into contracts, the arrangements under which organizations will perform services on their behalf must be made and continued on the basis of cooperation and good will among the parties involved.

2. Collaboratives can be created by local ordinance to act in an advisory capacity for local governments and communities on issues affecting the well-being of children and their families. Local governments have the authority to create, by ordinance, advisory bodies. The ordinances creating these collaboratives will define their duties and responsibilities. In addition, these ordinances will specify the number of members these collaboratives will have, the qualifications and terms of office of the members, the frequency with which the collaboratives will meet, and the officers they will have and their terms of office. These ordinances can require such collaboratives to work with and through designated departments of local government.

Advisory collaboratives created by ordinances can adopt bylaws. These bylaws must be consistent with the provisions of the ordinances that created them. Bylaws can be adopted to establish rules of procedure for meeting, specify the number of terms the officers can serve, and address other "housekeeping" issues, including the procedures for amending the bylaws.

Unless authorized by state law, local governments cannot grant legal powers to advisory collaboratives. However, local governments can assign them responsibility for assisting in the development of plans to address the problems of children and their families. Advisory collaboratives can also be assigned responsibility for reviewing and submitting recommendations for allocating funds or entering into contracts to implement the strategies contained in the plans. Finally, advisory collaboratives can be assigned responsibility for reporting to the community on the condition of children and their families and on the progress being made in helping them.

Although advisory collaboratives have no legal powers, the local governments that create them do. Local governments can adopt and help implement the plans recommended by these collaboratives; they have the power to enter into contracts, receive and spend money, and employ staff. Local governments have the authority to enter into multiyear contracts with other units of government and annual contracts with private, nonprofit organizations. Local governments can receive and match federal grants as well as receive gifts of money and property. In addition, they can adopt policies and enact ordinances and regulations to implement the plans for helping children and families. Moreover, local governments have the authority to provide many of the services that may be called for by these plans.

Legal Powers of Collaboratives

Collaboratives created under the authority of legislation or incorporation charters can be granted legal powers. These powers will be specified in either the legislation or the incorporation charters. The scope of these powers can vary. However, under the provisions of the

Georgia Policy Council for Children and Families Act, a collaborative seeking to become a Community Partnership must have at least the following powers:[2]

1. To have a seal and alter the same at its pleasure;

2. To acquire, hold, and dispose of in its own name by purchase, gift, lease, or exchange, on such terms and conditions and in such manner and by such instrument as it may deem proper, real and personal property of every kind, character, and description, but the community partnership shall not have the power to acquire any real or personal property by condemnation or eminent domain;

3. To procure insurance against any loss in connection with its property and other assets of the community partnership;

4. To make contracts and to execute all instruments necessary or convenient in connection therewith;

5. To adopt, alter, or repeal its own bylaws, rules, and regulations governing the manner in which its business may be transacted and in which the power granted to it may be enjoyed, as the community partnership may deem necessary and expedient in facilitating its business;

6. To receive, accept, and utilize gifts, grants, donations, or contributions of money, property, facilities, or services, with or without consideration, from any person, firm, corporation, foundation, or other entity or from this state (Georgia) or any agency, instrumentality, or political subdivision thereof or from the United States or any agency or instrumentality thereof;

7. To select, appoint, and employ professional, administrative, clerical, or other personnel and to contract for professional or other services and to allow suitable compensation for such personnel services; and

8. To do all things necessary and convenient to carry out the powers and purposes of the community partnership which are expressly provided for in this article.

Bylaws for Governing Collaboratives

Governing collaboratives will need rules and procedures for conducting their business. These should be formalized in bylaws adopted by the collaboratives. Bylaws should address such issues as the frequency, dates, and times for regular meetings; the rules of order that will be followed; and the procedures for electing officers, including the dates on which their terms of office will begin and end. The bylaws of collaboratives seeking to become Community Partnerships under the Policy Council Act must specify, in addition to other matters, the terms of office and succession of the members of a collaborative's governing body; the manner of selecting officers of that governing body and the terms and powers of such officers; a quorum (usually set at one-half of the membership of a board plus one additional member, a quorum can be higher but is rarely lower); the minimum meeting schedule; the reporting and financial audit requirements; and the compensation or reimbursements that will be paid to the members of the governing body.[3]

Bylaws adopted by collaboratives cannot grant powers that are not authorized by law or by incorporation charters. Usually these enabling laws or charters specify the officers the collaboratives must have, the membership of the collaboratives, and the method of appointing the members and their terms of office. In addi-

---

2. O.C.G.A., Article 12 of Chapter 5 of Title 49, Section 49-5-259.

3. O.C.G.A., Article 12 of Chapter 5 of Title 49, Section 49-5-259.

tion, these laws or charters usually specify the minimum frequency with which the collaboratives must meet and the quorum requirements for their meetings. Bylaws must conform to the requirements of the enabling laws or charters.

Membership of Collaboratives

Whatever form they take, collaboratives need members on their governing boards who are politically sophisticated, have power and influence, and are supported and respected in their community. In addition, these members should be able to gain the support and participation of all groups, individuals, and organizations in the community whose actions or inactions can affect the capacity of children to avoid or overcome barriers to success. Finally, the membership of collaboratives in Georgia should comply with the membership criteria for Community Partnerships specified in the Policy Council Act. These criteria call for the membership of a Community Partnership collaborative to include representatives from at least the following groups:

- Local elected officials of governing bodies in the community. (Governing bodies include those of county governments, municipal governments, and public school districts.)
- Persons from the business community.
- Persons from public agencies in the community that have ex officio members on the Georgia Policy Council for Children and Families (the Departments of Human Resources, Education, and Children and Youth Services), other than the Office of Planning and Budget.
- Members of boards of civic organizations.
- Members of the boards of private social service providers.
- Advocates for children and families.

The categories of members listed above are those required for Community Partnership

designation. (Meeting the membership requirements does not automatically qualify collaboratives to become Community Partnerships. To qualify, collaboratives must also have the legal powers and bylaws specified in the Georgia Policy Council Act.)

In addition to these membership categories, collaboratives can be strengthened by also including representatives from the following groups:

- County and municipal local government managers.
- School district superintendents.
- Leaders from neighborhoods experiencing social and economic problems.
- Executives from job training and job placement agencies.
- Leaders from neighborhood organizations and institutions.
- Users of public and private social service agencies.
- Representatives from the religious community.
- Members (or their appointees) of the local delegation to the House and Senate of the General Assembly.

Size of the Governing Boards

The size of the governing boards of collaboratives will be dictated in part by the number and categories of groups the creators of the collaboratives want to be represented on these boards. To ensure that most of the critical groups are represented, most collaboratives will need at least 15 members. Some will need more. However, care should be taken to keep these boards from becoming too large to be effective.

Method of Appointing Members

An issue that must be addressed is the method by which appointments to collaborative boards will be made. If collaboratives have been created under the authority of state enabling legislation, this legislation will specify the method of appointment. For example, this legislation might identify several appointing authorities including county governments, municipal governments, local school boards, local delegates to the General Assembly, and perhaps the heads of designated departments of state government. Further, this legislation usually will specify the number of appointments each of the appointing authorities can make.

If collaboratives have been created under the authority of incorporation charters, these charters will specify the method that will be used to appoint members. For private, non-profit organizations, responsibility for appointing members is usually limited to the organization and is not shared by other public or private bodies.

For advisory collaboratives created by ordinance, the ordinance will specify the method of appointment. Usually, this ordinance will specify that the appointments be made by the local governments that created these collaboratives.

Members are not appointed to meet-and-confer groups. Instead, individuals, agencies, and organizations are invited to participate by other individuals, agencies, and organizations. These invitations can be accepted or rejected. If accepted, the invitees decide for themselves how long they will participate in the group.

Involving Others

In addition to the appointed members of their governing boards, collaboratives may want other individuals and organizations to participate. Collaboratives can obtain this participation by (1) appointing persons to their boards as nonvoting, ex officio members, or (2) appointing persons to their working committees.

These committees can include board members as well as others from the community. In addition, they can include staff persons from various agencies and organizations who can bring special knowledge and skills to the work of the committees.

Purposes of Collaboratives

Whatever form the collaborative takes, its purposes for being created should be specified. If a collaborative is created by legislation, the legislation should specify its purposes. If created by incorporation charter, the charter should specify its purposes. If created by ordinance, the ordinance should specify its purposes. For meet-and-confer collaboratives, the participants should sign a joint declaration, specifying the purposes for which the participants are meeting.

Ideally, the purposes of collaboratives should be as follows:

- To develop community-supported visions and related goals for children and their families.
- To develop, adopt, amend, and advocate a comprehensive plan to accomplish the goals and the visions.
- To manage the implementation of the plans and monitor their effectiveness in achieving the goals and the visions that have been adopted.
- When legally empowered to do so, to contract with public and private agencies to carry out the strategies and interventions specified in the plans.
- To gain the participation of agencies and institutions in carrying out the strategies and interventions specified in the plans.

In addition to these purposes, communities may wish to assign other purposes to their collaboratives. These are decisions each community must make. However, the Georgia

Policy Council Act has established purposes for Community Partnerships. Collaboratives seeking to become Community Partnerships should make sure their purposes are consistent with those listed in the Act.

Deciding What Form of Collaborative to Create

Of the four forms of collaboratives that have been described, those that have legal powers can be more powerful and effective advocates and activists for children than those with no legal powers. One reason for this is that these collaboratives have a level of independence not available to collaboratives with no legal powers. Another reason is that collaboratives with legal powers have the ability to contract for and to provide services. Those without legal powers cannot do these things.

However, the ability to exercise legal powers does not automatically make collaboratives powerful. Collaboratives must also have members with power and influence who will help them gain attention, support, and respect in the community. With the power that support and respect give them, collaboratives with legal powers can influence decisions on public policies and public funding that can help children. Without such support and respect, collaboratives will find that the legal powers they have will be of limited value in helping children.

In selecting a form, then, communities must decide whether or not they want their collaboratives to have legal powers. In addition, they must decide whether or not they want to include as collaborative members those who have power and influence in the community. Finally, they must decide whether or not they want their collaboratives to qualify as Community Partnerships under the provisions of the Georgia

Policy Council for Children and Families Act adopted by the General Assembly of Georgia in 1995. This Act is codified in the Official Code of Georgia Annotated, Sections 49-5-250 through 49-5-264.

Establishing a Vision and Developing a Plan to Achieve It

After a collaborative has been organized, it should adopt a vision statement that formally describes the ends to which all efforts will be directed. A *vision* is *a destination to be reached, a dream to be pursued.* It gives *direction and purpose to the planning and work of the collaborative.* Without a vision, the collaborative will be faced with the handicap aptly stated in the adage that "if you don't know where you are going, any route will get you there." Stated another way, if the collaborative does not know what it wants to achieve, then any plan will work.

Legal power does not automatically make collaboratives powerful.

One way for a collaborative to develop a vision is to describe the perfect world results it would like for all children to achieve. An example of a vision for children is that "all children will grow up to become successful, productive, and contributing adults."

The vision adopted by a collaborative should be one that is supported by the community and that the community helped develop. A vision should be stated in a form that can be used to monitor progress in achieving it.

After a collaborative adopts a vision statement, it must develop a plan that will guide and direct efforts to make the vision become a reality. Appendix A is a sample outline of a plan of work that lists the various tasks to be completed or issues to be addressed. Parties that will be responsible for completing each task also need to be identified in this schedule. The next seven chapters in this manual describe a step-by-step process that collaboratives can follow in developing a plan.

Discussion Questions

1. Do we need a collaborative in this community that can be an advocate and activist on behalf of children and their families? Why?

2. If we need a collaborative, what form should it take? Should it be a quasi-governmental organization? A private, nonprofit organization? An advisory body? A meet-and-confer group? Why is this form being selected?

3. Who should be on its governing board? What groups, organizations, and institutions should be represented on this board? Will local elected officials be represented? Will the business community be represented? Will civic clubs be represented? Will public and private social service agencies be represented? Will neighborhoods and families with social and economic problems be represented?

4. What purposes will the collaborative have?

5. What legal powers should it have?

6. What actions are needed to create the collaborative, and who will take the lead in creating it?

7. Should the collaborative be in a form that will meet the requirements for becoming a Community Partnership collaborative?

8. What should the collaborative's vision be?

3 Step 1 Adopting Goals
2 Determining Baseline Conditions
3 Identifying Risk Factors
4 Establishing Objectives
5 Designing and Executing Strategies
6 Budgeting
7 Monitoring and Evaluating

When collaboratives begin the process of developing their plans, they should start by adopting goals. These *goals* should specify *the ideal conditions that collaboratives believe must exist if their vision for children is to become a reality*. These goals will be the standards by which collaboratives compare the real world with the ideal. They will be the yardsticks by which collaboratives can determine whether or not conditions exist that will be obstacles to them in achieving their vision.

Although sometimes perceived otherwise, establishing goals is not unique to the planning process. Implicitly or explicitly, all of us "establish" standards, or goals, by which we define our concepts of a perfect world. We use these standards to make judgments

Goals should be yardsticks to measure ideals.

about the conditions we find in the real world. For example, an ideal or standard for most of us is that our community will be free of people sleeping on the streets. We may not consciously identify this as our ideal, but we unconsciously use it to make a judgment about the homeless people we see sleeping on streets and sidewalks, or in parks. The goals of collaboratives cannot be implicit, however; they must be explicit statements of the standards or ideals for the conditions that collaboratives believe must exist if the perfect world they envision is to become a reality.

To be useful, goals must be stated in a form that will permit collaboratives to use them as yardsticks to measure the extent to which the ideals are not being met. They must also be in a form that will permit collaboratives to measure progress in achieving them. Goals that do not meet these criteria are of no value to collaboratives in developing their plans. To illustrate, consider the goal that "all unwed teenage girls will be free of motherhood." This goal provides a standard that can be used as a yardstick to determine if a condition exists, and if it does, the extent to which it exists—that is, whether or not unwed teenage girls are having babies and the number and rate at which they are having babies. However, the goal "all children in a school system will be provided with a caring and supportive learning environment" does not provide a standard for determining the extent to which a "caring and supportive learning environment" exists or is missing in the school system. What is a "caring and supportive learning environment"? What are the criteria for determining if it exists? How can the extent to which it does not exist be measured? This goal, in the form that it is presented, offers no guidance in answering these questions.

Setting Goals for Children and Adolescents

In an ideal world, all children will grow up free of the success inhibiters that can prevent them from achieving successful adulthood. In establishing their goals, collaboratives should define the success inhibiters that children must avoid to enhance their prospects for becoming successful adults. If collaboratives find that not all children are free of these inhibiters, they can use these findings as the starting point to design strategies to reduce the number who are not free of them. These strategies must include interventions directed to children and their families. They must be designed to serve two purposes: (1) to help keep children free of success inhibiters, and (2) to help children who are experiencing success inhibiters overcome the obstacles to success that these inhibiters create.

In developing goals for children, collaboratives should avoid the temptation to adopt goals that address specific activities or performance. Such goals are easy to construct but are of no value in measuring the well-being of children in the community. For example, a collaborative that adopts a goal "to provide tutoring in math to 100 delinquent youth at the youth detention center" is adopting a process or work level it wants performed. It is describing a means to accomplish an end that is not defined. This goal does not describe an ideal condition that the collaborative would like to exist, and it does not provide a standard the collaborative can use to identify and measure math literacy conditions of youth in the detention center. Without this information, the collaborative has no way of deter-

mining if a problem exists and the extent to which it exists. In addition, it has no standard for measuring progress in reducing the problem.

Instead, an appropriate goal might be that "all youth 16 years of age and under will have grade-appropriate math literacy rates equal to or greater than the national average for grade-appropriate math literacy." With this standard, the collaborative can determine whether youth in the detention center meet this standard and on the basis of this finding decide what changes should be made. The strategy might be to provide a math literacy tutoring program for 100 youth in the center. However, the measure of success would be the progress made in the math literacy levels of the students in the tutoring program rather than the number of youth served by the program.

In developing goals, collaboratives should also avoid the temptation to establish goals that address risk factors. For example, a risk factor for unsuccessful school performance can be lack of parental involvement in the school life of children. A strategy—not a goal—will address this risk factor. The goal should not be that all parents will be involved in the school life of their children. Rather, the goal should be that all children will succeed in school. However, a strategy to help reduce the number of children who are not succeeding in school might be directed to increasing the involvement of parents in the school life of their children.

Collaboratives should also avoid goals that address strategies. For example, a strategy that might be used to help prepare children for school would be to place children in quality preschool child care programs. The goal should not be to place children in quality child care. The goal should be that all children will enter school with the cognitive skills needed to succeed in school.

Examples of Goals

When establishing goals, collaboratives should consider adopting a continuum of goals. This continuum will provide "mileposts" that can be used to monitor and measure the condition of children in their progressive stages of development. The continuum can also be used by collaboratives to monitor their accomplishments in keeping children free of the success inhibiters and in mitigating the effects of these inhibiters on the children already experiencing them. A continuum of goals for children should begin with birth and continue to adulthood. It might read as follows:

Sample Goals for Children, Ages 0–10

- All infants will survive birth and the first year of life.
- All infants will be born with normal birthweights.
- All children will remain free of preventable diseases and uncorrected, but correctable, handicaps.
- All children will remain free of abuse and neglect.
- All children will progress through elementary school without being overage for grade and without being retained in grade, beginning in the first grade.
- All children, beginning in the first grade, will equal or exceed the standard for mastery of grade-level reading, math, and language skills.

Sample Goals for Adolescents, Ages 11–19

- All adolescents will progress through middle school and high school without being retained and without being overage for grade.
- All adolescents will graduate from high school on time with twelfth-grade level reading, math, and language skills.

- All female adolescents will remain free of unwed parenthood.
- All unwed adolescent mothers will remain free of further births and will graduate from high school with twelfth-grade level reading, math, and language skills.
- All adolescents will remain free of criminal delinquency.
- All out-of-school adolescents will be free of unemployment and inactivity.
- All adolescents will remain free of violent deaths.

Another way of listing goals is by categories of well-being. For example, the preceding goals can be categorized as follows:

Health and Safety

- All infants will survive birth and the first year of life.
- All infants will be born with normal birthweights.
- All children will remain free of preventable diseases and uncorrected, but correctable, handicaps.
- All children will remain free of abuse and neglect.

School Success

- All children will progress through school without being overage for grade and without being retained in grade, beginning in the first grade.
- All children, beginning in the first grade, will equal or exceed the standard for mastery of grade-level reading, math, and language skills.
- All adolescents will progress through school without being retained and without being overage for grade.
- All adolescents will graduate from high school on time with twelfth-grade level reading, math, and language skills.

Social Well-Being

- All female adolescents will remain free of unwed parenthood.
- All unwed adolescent mothers will remain free of further births and will graduate from high school with twelfth-grade level reading, math, and language skills.
- All adolescents will remain free of criminal delinquency.
- All out-of-school adolescents will be free of unemployment and inactivity.
- All adolescents will remain free of violent deaths.

Repeat Incidents

- All children will remain free of experiencing repeat occurrences of success inhibiters such as grade retention, unwed pregnancies, and delinquency.

Developing Useful Goals

Collaboratives will discover during the planning process that developing meaningful and useful goals—goals which define the success inhibiters that children and youth should be free of—will not be easy. This effort can be made easier if collaboratives will remind themselves that the adults who are committing crimes and violence, who are in prison, who are unemployed and unemployable, who are on welfare, and who are creating the public disorders that blight neighborhoods and frighten people did not start life as adults. They started life as infants. As they progressed from infancy to adulthood, protective supports were missing in their lives. Without these supports, they were unable to avoid or overcome the negative conditions that influenced them to become unsuccessful and unproductive adults. The challenge for collaboratives is to determine what these negative conditions are and to establish goals that call for children to be free of them.

In developing their goals, collaboratives must seek the participation and concurrence of all agencies, organizations, institutions, and individuals in the community who, in turn, must support the work of the collaboratives. Collaboratives must also seek the participation and concurrence of all agencies and organizations in the community who can provide the services and interventions necessary to accomplish the goals. If they do not gain this participation and concurrence when adopting their goals, then there is very little chance that collaboratives will be successful in their efforts to help children become successful adults.

The adults who are committing crimes and creating public disorders did not start life as adults.

Discussion Questions

1. What is a goal?
2. What conditions should a goal address?
3. How should goals be structured?
4. What are the goals for children in our community?
5. Do these goals address success inhibiters? If not, what do they address?
6. Are our goals stated in a form that will permit us to use them as a standard to measure the condition of children in the community? If not, how can they be modified to do this?

After collaboratives adopt their goals, they next should determine the *baseline conditions* for the community. *Baseline conditions* are *measurements of the numbers and rates of children in the community who are not meeting the goals.* These measurements document, at a given point in time, how many children are experiencing barriers that can inhibit their ability to become successful adults. The challenge for collaboratives is to develop strategies that, over time, will reduce these baseline numbers. After the strategies have been implemented, collaboratives can use the baseline numbers to monitor progress in reducing these numbers.

Measuring the Baseline Conditions

When measuring baseline conditions, collaboratives should either select a base year for making these measurements or, when appropriate, select a multiyear period for calculating the average rates and numbers for the conditions being measured. When possible, collaboratives should break down the measurements by age, race, gender, and neighborhood. This breakdown will help identify the groups of children who have the highest rates for falling short in meeting the goals. This information can be used by collaboratives to establish priorities and targets for action.

The benefit of breaking down data to show the differences in the rates and numbers among the children of a community is illustrated in the following tables. In this example, the goal that is the basis for these baseline measurements is that "all teenage girls will remain free

of births." Table 1 shows that this goal is not being met and shows as a total, or aggregate number and rate, the extent to which it is not being met. However, the data in this table do not identify the groups of teenage girls who are experiencing the highest birthrates. Table 2 breaks down, or disaggregates, these data by age and race. From this table, the groups of teenage girls with the highest birthrates can be identified. Collaboratives that break down their baseline data into appropriate groupings for each of their goals, in the manner illustrated in Table 2, will be in a better position to target their interventions than collaboratives that do not do this.[1]

Table 1 shows that the aggregate birthrate for births to unwed teenage girls was 45.69 per

TABLE 1		
Large County, Georgia Number and Rate of Births to Unwed Teenage Girls, 1995		
Group	Number of Births	Birthrate (per 1,000)
Unwed teenage girls	718	45.69

---

1. The data for the tables presented in this chapter were obtained from several sources. These data are used only to provide examples of baseline condition measurements. Although these data represent real conditions, the communities these data measure are not identified. They are termed "Large County" or "Medium County" for illustrative purposes.

TABLE 2		
Large County, Georgia **Number and Rate of Births** **to Unwed Teenage Girls, by Age and Race, 1995**		
Group	Number of Births	Birthrate (per 1,000)
Ages 10–19	718	45.69
White	211	27.07
African American	507	64.00
Ages 10–14	32	4.10
White	1	.30
African American	31	7.80
Ages 15–17	308	64.90
White	69	29.00
African American	239	100.90
Ages 18–19	382	120.70
White	141	88.90
African American	237	150.20

duce the aggregate birthrate for unwed teen-age girls from 45.69 to 27.00 per 1,000 girls in the 10- to 19-year age group, it would need to give priority attention to the group with a rate of 64.00 per 1,000 to achieve this objective rather than the group with a rate of 27.07 per 1,000.

What Baseline Conditions Measure— and What They Don't

Baseline conditions measure the number of children in the community who are already experiencing one or more of the success inhibiters specified in the goals. Baseline conditions *do not* measure the number of children who are free of these inhibiters but who may be vulnerable to experiencing them. Collaboratives need to determine the number of children who fall into each of these groups.

For the children who are already experiencing inhibiters, collaboratives require the baseline numbers to know how many children and their families need corrective and preventive help, or interventions, and pro-

1,000 girls in this group.[2] However, when the data in Table 1 are disaggregated as shown in Table 2, a different picture emerges. Table 2 shows that some groups of teenage girls are experiencing much higher birthrates than others.

By breaking down the data in the manner illustrated in Table 2, collaboratives can identify the groups in greatest need of help. They can also determine which groups to target to produce the greatest improvement in the aggregate baseline rates. For example, if a collaborative established an objective to re-

Baseline conditions do not measure the number of children who are free of success inhibiters but may be vulnerable to them.

---

2. Birthrate is defined as the total births to females in an age group divided by the number of females in the age group and multiplied by 1,000. For example 718 babies were born to teenage girls ages 10–19. There are 15,713 girls in this age group. Therefore: $718/15,713 \times 1,000 =$ a rate of 45.69.

tective support. For the children who are not yet experiencing the inhibiters but who are vulnerable to them, collaboratives need estimates of the number in this group to determine the resources that will be required to provide preventive and protective interventions to these children and their families.

The number of children who are experiencing success inhibiters can be found in vital statistics reports, student performance reports, census reports, and other statistical reports on the condition of children. However, data are not readily available for the number of children who are free of the success inhibiters but who are vulnerable to them. These numbers must be estimated. To make these estimates, collaboratives must identify conditions that make children vulnerable and then estimate the number who are exposed to these conditions.

Examples of Baseline Conditions

The following are examples of baseline condition measurements. These are presented to illustrate the value of disaggregating data and the value of measuring different stages of development. The conditions used in these examples are low birthweights, births to unwed teenage girls, school performance, and abuse and neglect. To make these examples more useful, goals are stated, then the conditions to be measured are identified, and finally, examples of baseline numbers and rates are presented.

Low birthweight

Goal: All infants will be born free of low birthweights.

Condition to be measured: Number and rate for low birthweight babies.

Baseline conditions: See Table 3.

TABLE 3			
Medium County, Georgia **Number and Percentage of Low Birthweight** **Births, by Age and Race of Mother, 1994**			
Age and Race of Mother	**Total Births**	**Number of Low Birthweight Births**	**Percentage of Total Births**
Adult mothers	754	69	9.2
White	512	37	7.2
African American	242	32	13.2
Ages 15–17	73	11	15.1
White	34	3	8.8
African American	39	8	20.5
Ages 18–19	118	11	9.3
White	63	4	6.3
African American	55	7	12.7

A number of studies report that low birthweight is a risk factor for behavior problems and learning problems. These studies have also found that with the proper attention and support, children with these problems can be helped. As Table 3 shows, one group of children has much higher rates for low birthweights than the other group. The children in the group with the higher rates may be the same children who will lack the attention and support they need to avoid behavior and learning problems. By disaggregating and evaluating this data in conjunction with other data, collaboratives can ensure that appropriate priority is given to the group of children in greatest need of help.

Births to unwed teenage mothers

Goal: All unwed teenage girls will remain free of first births or repeat births.

Condition to be measured: First births and repeat births to unwed teenage girls.

Baseline conditions: See Table 4.

Often, when collaboratives address the issue of births to unwed teenage girls, they do not consider that some of the births are first births and some are repeat births. As a result, they adopt strategies to reduce the total birthrate that seem to assume that all births are first births, when in fact this is not the case (see Table 4). Failure to recognize this can result in strategies producing little or no benefit. Obviously, girls who are vulnerable to having a second or third child are much easier to identify and target than girls who are vulnerable to first births. This means that collaboratives may have more success in reducing repeat births than in reducing first births and, therefore, more success in reducing the birthrates than if they focus only on first births. However, collaboratives will not have the information to proceed in this way if they do not address the fact that birthrates are made up of first births *and* repeat births. Further, they will not be able to target the most vulnerable groups without the type of breakdown illustrated in Table 4.

School performance

Goal: All students who enter the ninth grade will graduate from high school on time.

Condition to be measured: Percentage of students who enter the ninth grade but do not enter the twelfth grade four years later and do not graduate by the end of the school year.

Baseline conditions: See Table 5.

Children who are not succeeding in school do not encounter problems for the first time in the ninth grade. These problems are reflected much earlier in the form of grade retention rates and/or reading, math, or other learning achievement standards. Retention problems can begin to appear in the early grades and become more serious as children progress through the grades. Table 6 illustrates this condition. It also shows the differences in retention rates among the groups of students in the school system, which means collaboratives can better target their efforts.

TABLE 4
Large County, Georgia **Number and Rate of First Births and Repeat Births** **to Teenage Girls, by Age and Race, 1994**

	First Births		Repeat Births	
Age and Race of Mother	**Number**	**Rate (per 1,000)**	**Number**	**Rate (per 1,000)**
Ages 15–17				
White	43	13.6	13	4.0
African American	134	47.8	42	15.0
Ages 18–19				
White	45	20.2	26	10.3
African American	100	50.4	101	51.0

TABLE 5
Large County, Georgia **Percentage of Students Entering the Ninth Grade** **Who Did Not Graduate on Time, by Race,** **Graduation School Year 1995–96**

Group	Graduated	Transferred	Did Not Graduate[a]
All Students	38.2	18.3	43.5
White	38.3	20.6	41.1
African American	38.6	16.5	44.9

[a] Retained or dropped out.

TABLE 6

Large County, Georgia
Percentage of Students Retained for Select Grades,
by Gender and Race, School Year 1994–95

Gender and Race	Grade Level			
	Kinder-garten	First	Sixth	Ninth
Male				
White	2.9	6.8	8.1	32.5
African American	3.4	9.8	11.2	43.3
Female				
White	1.2	4.9	2.6	23.3
African American	2.2	7.0	6.8	30.9

cern collaboratives. However, they illustrate the process by which properly structured goals can help identify and measure problems and establish baseline conditions. These examples also illustrate the need to break down or disaggregate data to provide as much clarity as possible about the characteristics of the children who are experiencing the success inhibiters and to identify the groups of children who have the most urgent need for help.

Abuse and neglect

Goal: All children will be free of abuse and neglect.

Condition to be measured: The number of confirmed cases of child abuse and neglect.

Baseline conditions: See Table 7.

Table 7 is presented as an example of baseline data that is not complete. To be useful, this table should include data about the age and gender of the children who are being abused and neglected. This table should also include the number and rate of first-time incidents and repeat incidents. These data are available in the records of the agencies that deal with abuse and neglect. In most instances, however, such data must be retrieved manually. As a result, organizations frequently do not obtain this information. Without it, targeted interventions for addressing abuse and neglect cannot be designed.

The examples in this chapter do not cover all of the success inhibiters that will con-

Gathering Baseline Data

Most, if not all, of the baseline data needed by collaboratives are available by county—and sometimes by neighborhood—in the records of organizations that serve children. If all of these organizations commit themselves to

TABLE 7

Medium County, Georgia
Number of Confirmed Cases
of Child Abuse and Neglect, by Race, 1994

Case	Total	White	African American
Neglect	501	276	183
Physical Abuse	172	74	89
Sexual Abuse	57	37	18
Emotional Abuse	57	36	16
Other	27	16	9
Total	814	439	315
Rate (per 1,000 children under age 18)	15.8	14.9	16.6

		TABLE 8		
	Sources of Local Baseline Data for Aggregated and Disaggregated Rates and Numbers			
Condition	**Source of Data**	**Aggregated Data**	**Disaggregated Data**
Infant mortality Low birthweight births	*Vital Statistics Reports,* Georgia Department of Human Resources, Health Assessment Services	Yes	Yes
Unwed teenage pregnancy	County Departments of Health	Yes	Yes
Unwed teenage births, first births, and repeat births	*Georgia County Guide,* Cooperative Extension Service, University of Georgia	Yes	Partially
	Benchmark Data, Georgia Policy Council for Children and Families	Yes	Not yet
	Georgia Kids Count Factsheet, Georgians for Children	Yes (except repeat births)	Yes (except repeat births)
Juvenile Delinquency	Juvenile Court	Yes	Yes
Juvenile Arrest	*Benchmark Data,* Georgia Policy Council for Children and Families	Yes	Not yet
	Georgia County Guide, Cooperative Extension Service, University of Georgia	Yes	Partially
Child Abuse	Department of Family and Children Services	Yes	Partially
	Georgia Kids Count Factsheet, Georgians for Children	Yes	Yes
	Benchmark Data, Georgia Policy Council for Children and Families	Yes	Not yet
School performance, by grade • Failure rates • Retention rates • Overage-for-grade rates • Math and reading scores • In-school and out-of-school suspensions • Drop-out rates • Graduation rates	Local School System	Yes	Yes
	Georgia County Guide, Cooperative Extension Service, University of Georgia	Yes (limited)	No
	Benchmark Data, Georgia Policy Council for Children and Families	Yes (limited)	Not yet

working together to help children become successful adults, then collecting the data should not be difficult. Each of the organizations, with a little staff effort, can make its local data available in the detail needed for planning purposes. Some of the local organizations and agencies in communities that can provide local data appear in Table 8.

Table 8 identifies the sources of aggregated and disaggregated data.[3] Some of these sources can break down data by street address. Collaboratives can use these addresses to prepare spot maps that graphically show the concentrations of children who are experiencing success inhibiters or who are vulnerable to them. Collaboratives can use these maps in their

planning and in making presentations to the community about the condition of children. (For examples of spot maps, see pages 39-44.)

Discussion Questions

1. Do the goals of the collaborative provide standards for identifying and measuring the problems being experienced by children in the community?

2. Can we obtain data broken down by age, gender, and race for making baseline measurements?

3. Are these data available from the records of local agencies?

4. Will local agencies that have these data make them available to the collaborative?

5. If these data are not available locally, from what source(s) will the collaborative obtain them?

6. How will we assemble the data we need?

---

3. Other sources of data can be found in the 1996 publication, *Aiming for Results: A Guide to Georgia's Benchmarks for Children and Families* (Atlanta: Georgia Policy Council on Children and Families).

5

1 **Adopting Goals**
2 **Determining Baseline Conditions**
Step 3 Identifying Risk Factors
4 **Establishing Objectives**
5 **Designing and Executing Strategies**
6 **Budgeting**
7 **Monitoring and Evaluating**

To help children become successful and contributing adults, they need supportive and caring parents, socially and environmentally healthy neighborhoods, and attentive and responsive community service agencies. These are called *protective factors* and are defined as *conditions in the lives of children that enable them to avoid or overcome the success inhibitors that can be barriers to achieving successful adulthood.* Protective factors include the following:

- Families in which children feel connected and close to and are cared for by family members. Such families consist of parents or significant other adults who provide protection and support for their children, encourage and facilitate the development of their cognitive and motor skills, and motivate and mentor them to keep them free of conditions that can harm their prospects for success.

- Neighborhoods to which children are connected that are physically safe and environmentally clean and healthy and that provide children with positive role models, and supportive and protective neighbors and neighborhood institutions.

- Peers with whom children are connected who reinforce the positive values and motivations children learn from their families and neighbors.

- Schools that children enjoy attending and that provide them with a sense of belonging.

- Community institutions and services that reinforce and strengthen the values, skills, and motivations children learn from their families.

- Families that do not experience the stress of parental unemployment, poverty, domestic violence, and parental substance abuse.

- Two-parent families.

- Innate capacities that enable some children to overcome the effects of family stress conditions.

Children who have these protective factors at work in their lives are less likely to experience success inhibitors than those children who do not. These protective factors appear to work in ways that help to keep children free of the negative impacts of risk conditions even when they are exposed to them.

Protective factors are missing in the lives of many children. As a consequence, these chil-

Protective factors help keep children free of the negative impacts of risk conditions.

dren may not receive the protective help they need to avoid or overcome success inhibiters such as unwed teenage motherhood, juvenile delinquency, and school failure. The conditions that can make children vulnerable to success inhibiters are called *risk factors* in this manual. *Risk factors* are defined *as the absence of protective factors.*

Risk factors produce the environments that make children vulnerable to experiencing success inhibiters. The challenge collaboratives face is that of identifying these risk factors and designing appropriate strategies to mitigate or remove them. Collaboratives must meet this challenge successfully if they are to be effective in reducing the baseline conditions they find. For example, what are the risk factors that can make children vulnerable to becoming delinquents? What strategies and interventions can be used to mitigate or remove these risk factors?

Categorizing Risk Factors

Children can be confronted with a variety of risk factors that make them vulnerable to success inhibiters. These risk factors can be grouped into the following categories:

• Pre-birth risk factors.
• Individual risk factors.
• Family risk factors.
• Neighborhood risk factors.
• Economic risk factors.
• Service delivery risk factors.
• Success inhibiters.

Pre-birth Risk Factors

Pre-birth risk factors are preventable conditions that mothers incur during pregnancy. These factors can create birth problems such as infant mortality, low birthweight, drug de-

pendency syndromes, and other conditions that can become risk factors for the healthy development of children. Pre-birth risk factors that can harm children include the following:

a. Inadequate prenatal care for expectant mothers.
b. Expectant mothers who use and abuse drugs, tobacco, and alcohol before and during pregnancy.
c. Expectant mothers who have preventable diseases that they pass on to their unborn children.
d. Expectant mothers who are in poor health and pass on this condition to their unborn children.
e. Expectant mothers who suffer from inadequate nutrition during their pregnancy.

Individual Risk Factors

Individual risk factors are characteristics which, if not mitigated by effective protective support, can cause children to experience success inhibiters. These factors include the following:

a. Low birthweight.
b. Learning disabilities.
c. Hearing and vision problems.
d. Physical and mental health problems.
e. Aggressive and rebellious behavior.
f. Cognitive development problems.
g. Early childhood drug and alcohol dependency.

Family Risk Factors

Family risk factors are the *absence* of protective supports that can help prevent children from becoming susceptible to success inhibiters. From their families, children need health and nutritional care and help in developing cognitive and learning skills. In addition, they need support, assistance, and moti-

**Children need
positive experiences, role models,
values, and motivations.**

vation to help them succeed in school. Also, they need to be protected from abuse, neglect, and violence. Finally, they need positive experiences, role models, values, and motivations to help keep them free of delinquency, drug abuse, and unwed parenthood. When protective factors are missing in their lives, children may not be able to avoid or overcome success inhibiters such as school failure, delinquent conduct, or teenage parenthood. The types of families in which these protective supports are often missing include the following:

a. Families headed by adult unwed mothers who may have been unwed teenage mothers. They may also be school dropouts and may provide little or no positive support to their children that could help them succeed in school.

b. Families in which sibling sisters may be unwed teenage mothers and school dropouts.

c. Families headed by mothers who may not respond to acts of abuse to their children by boyfriends or other adults.

d. Families in which adults abuse their children rather than protect them from abuse.

e. Families in which one or both parents or other family adults abuse drugs and alcohol rather than serve as models for remaining free of drug and alcohol abuse.

f. A family environment in which adult members may resort to violent resolutions of conflicts rather than nonviolent resolutions.

g. A family environment in which the parents are unskilled in parenting and may be unable to help their children develop learning skills, positive values, and motivations. Further, they may be unable to provide them with the help and guidance needed to keep them free of disruptive behavior, school failure, delinquent behavior, unwed parenthood, and other problems.

h. A family environment in which the parent or parents are unemployed.

i. A family environment of living in poverty.

Neighborhood Risk Factors

Neighborhood risk factors are conditions in neighborhoods that can work to the detriment of vulnerable children. The following conditions are risk factors:

a. Neighborhood residents lack the social cohesion and concern that is needed to care for the neighborhood and its children.

b. Many people in the neighborhood are negative role models for the children.

c. Generally, people in the neighborhood are not working together to create and maintain a safe, clean, and supportive environment for children.

d. Churches, schools, and social service agencies in these neighborhoods do not always take an active and supportive interest in the well-being of children.

e. Agencies, organizations, and institutions serving these neighborhoods are not providing services that mitigate or remove risk factors affecting neighborhood children by creating or strengthening protective factors for these children. Institutions such as libraries, recreation centers, and churches in these neighborhoods may not reach out to serve children and families in need.

f. Services provided to these neighborhoods by local governments do not effectively and sufficiently address the problems of public disorders, infrastructure deficiencies, and deterioration and physical blight problems in the neighborhoods.

g. Neighborhoods have high concentrations of families living in poverty and high concentrations of unemployment and underemployment. They often have concentrations of female-headed, single-parent households, unwed teenage mothers, and adults who have not completed high school. Sometimes they have high rates of public disorders such as drunk-on-the street, family violence, loitering, loud noise, simple and aggravated assaults, crime, and drug trafficking.

h. Streets, lanes, yards, and vacant lots in these neighborhoods are littered with trash and debris and have high concentrations of both vacant and occupied dilapidated structures. These conditions are made worse by streets and sidewalks in poor repair; untended tree lawns and public landscaping; and inadequate amenities, such as parks and playgrounds.

Spot maps can be used to analyze the neighborhood environments of at-risk children and their families. These maps can show the areas in which such children are concentrated and where social and economic problems are concentrated. Often, these maps will demonstrate and confirm that there is a connection. Examples of spot maps that show these relationships are found on pages 39 through 44. These maps display conditions in the Savannah-Chatham County community and were prepared as a part of the data collection for the

work of the Savannah-Chatham County Youth Futures Authority.

The spot maps for the Savannah-Chatham County community show that the neighborhoods with the highest concentrations of children in distress are also the neighborhoods with the highest concentrations of social, physical, and child health problems. The maps demonstrate that there is a relationship between the risk factors in neighborhoods and the distribution of children who are experiencing success inhibiters.

Maps 1, 2, and 3 show where children who are experiencing success inhibiters are located in the community. Map 1 shows the distribution of abused and neglected children. Map 2 shows the distribution of births to unwed teenage girls. Map 3 shows the distribution of students in the sixth grade who are in the lowest percentile in reading skills.

Maps 4, 5, and 6 show characteristics of the neighborhoods in which the children who are experiencing the success inhibiters are concentrated. Map 4 shows the distribution of aggravated assaults in the community. Map 5 shows the distribution of children in the sixth grade from female-headed households. Map 6 shows the distribution of dilapidated housing.

From spot maps like these, collaboratives can also identify the locations where children who are not yet experiencing the success inhibiters but who are the most vulnerable to these inhibiters may be concentrated. These findings can be used to develop neighborhood interventions that help vulnerable children avoid these inhibiters.

Geographic Information System (GIS) technology can be used to prepare spot maps similar to the ones illustrated here. This technology can be found in most communities in Georgia and may be available from Regional Development Centers, planning departments, county or city engineering departments, regional public health agencies, or public utility departments. Agencies and organizations with operational GIS systems will have base maps of the communities they serve. If requested to help, many of these agencies and organizations will contribute to the work of the collaboratives by preparing spot maps. However, collaboratives will need to supply those preparing spot maps with the street address or block address locations of data they wish to have recorded. For example, street address or block address data are available in most communities for abused children, unwed teenage mothers, juveniles arrested for delinquency, or students who are overage for grade. Also available is information on the locations of substandard housing and deteriorated infrastructure, and on the distribution of crime.

Economic Risk Factors

Economic risk factors are the economic conditions of families that affect their ability to provide some of the protective supports needed for their children. A disproportionate number of the children who are in trouble come from families who live in poverty rather than from families with moderate to middle incomes. Children living in poverty often have higher rates of school failure, delinquency, unwed parenthood, and health problems. The reason that children living in poverty may be susceptible to success inhibiters is that their families may not be able to pay for the kinds of help and support they need to help them avoid or overcome these inhibiters. Children living in poverty may be unable to receive adequate health care. They may be unable to participate in enriching social and cultural activities that can help build values for success and social conduct. They may be unable to attend the kinds of day care facilities that can help them develop the learning skills needed for success in school. They may be unable to obtain the transportation to and from agencies adminis-

tering health care and social services. Finally, they may be unable to participate in planned and supervised recreational activities or to receive remedial tutoring when they are failing in school. When these supports are absent, children are vulnerable to success inhibiters.

Factors that can lead families into poverty or keep them in poverty include the following:

a. Parents who lack literacy levels or job skills to compete for jobs.

b. Single parents who cannot afford child care services during work hours.

c. Transportation costs that limit access to jobs.

d. Underemployment for wages that are too low to provide adequately for the needs of the family.

e. Vulnerability of employed, low-skilled parents to loss of jobs during economic downturns.

Service Delivery Risk Factors

Children and their families need service agencies to help them obtain relief from crises and to help them avoid crisis conditions. They need agencies that serve them as whole persons and families rather than as persons and families made up of individual parts unrelated to one another. Finally, children and their families need agencies to be a part of a service delivery system that provides a continuum of coordinated and complementary services to help these children avoid or overcome success inhibiters. The present structures for serving children and their families do not meet these criteria. They fall short in several ways:

a. *Lack of a coordinated, comprehensive, and integrated system of service delivery.* Agencies tend to provide categorical services to children rather than coordinated and comprehensive services. For example, children may have mental health problems, physical health problems, abuse and neglect problems, behavior problems, school failure problems, and nutritional problems. These conditions are often interrelated and need to be addressed with interventions that are complementary and coordinated. Often, however, the legal or collaborative arrangements needed to provide such services are not available. One agency is responsible for serving the mental health needs of children, another for serving physical health needs, another for providing welfare assistance, another for responding to child abuse and neglect, and another for providing education. Agencies do not consult with one another or plan together to provide a continuum of complementary services to clients. If agencies refer clients to other agencies, they rarely follow through to determine what happened to them. Further, agencies do not share collective responsibility for the well-being of the clients they serve.

Few agencies share client lists or client assessment information, and many duplicate one another's services, overhead costs, and record keeping. In addition, agencies often are separated by distance so that clients must travel to several different locations to be served. This fragmented and categorical delivery of services can and does work to the detriment of children and their families and is a risk factor that must be recognized and addressed, but often is not.

b. *Inability of agencies to provide prevention services.* The service programs of most agencies are designed to serve people in crisis situations, not to prevent the crisis from developing in the first place or to prevent it from recurring after relief or help has been provided. For example, in response to the problem of pregnant teenage students dropping out of school, an agency may establish a program to keep teenagers in school during their pregnancies. The program is successful in accomplishing this objective. However, after the teenagers deliver their babies, they are released from the program and no further initiatives are taken to ensure that the teenagers complete school and remain free of further pregnancies while still teenagers.

c. *Failure of agencies to place priority on achieving results.* The annual reports of many social service agencies list the number of clients served rather than the outcomes produced. Few agencies report on the results of their services and the percentage and number of clients whose lives were improved. Further, few agencies provide information about the rate and number of clients who remain permanently free of the problems or the rate and number who experience a recurrence of the problems.

Most agencies are designed to serve people in crisis, not to prevent the crisis in the first place.

d. *Inability of agencies to obtain waivers of mandates and procedures that prevent the coordination and integration of services.* A variety of public and private agencies provide services to children. However, various state and federal mandates, procedures, and grant restrictions create barriers to coordinating and integrating these services. As a result, children often receive fragmented, duplicated, and uncoordinated services that are impersonal and unresponsive to their needs.

e. *Capacity limitations that prevent agencies from providing both crisis intervention services and preventive intervention services.* The mission of most service agencies is to serve people who are in a crisis situation. Agencies fulfill this mission. However, the demand for crisis services is usually far greater than agencies' capacity to serve. Consequently, agencies usually have neither the flexibility nor the resources to provide or promote strategies for children and families to prevent problems or prevent their recurrence.

f. *Lack of convenient access and client-friendly admission procedures for services.* The location of service agencies and their hours of operation often make services too inconvenient or too costly for those who need them. These location barriers become greater problems if children and their families need multiple services, each of which is at a different location in the community. In addition to location barriers, agencies and institutions may have troublesome admission procedures that further hinder those needing help. An even greater barrier emerges if children and their families seeking help must visit several different agencies, each with its own admission procedures.

Success Inhibiters

The interaction between success inhibiters and risk factors is such that success inhibiters in themselves can act as risk factors. An example is school failure, which is both a success inhibiter and a risk factor.

Discovering Risk Factors in the Lives of Children

There is no way to identify with certainty the risk factors in the lives of children who are experiencing success inhibiters. However, if there is to be any success in correcting or preventing these inhibiters, these risk factors must be identified and controlled.

Collaboratives undertaking the task of identifying risk factors in the lives of children can approach this task in several ways. They can—

1. Review published research that reports the relationships found between the success inhibiters experienced by children and the risk factors to which they are exposed. Collaboratives can use these findings as a starting point for identifying the risk factors in the lives of the children they will target for interventions.

2. Assess the family and neighborhood conditions under which troubled children are living. Through this process, collaboratives can identify both the risk factors and protective factors that are at work in the lives of children.

3. Assess children and their families individually to identify any congenital risk factors these children have, and the presence or absence of protective factors and other risk factors in their lives.

4. Consult with agencies, organizations, and individuals that work with children who have problems and their families. These sources can identify both the protective factors and risk factors that exist in the lives of children.

Regardless of when they start identifying risk factors, collaboratives will discover that the risk factors found in the lives of the children they propose to target will fall into one or more of the categories identified earlier. The challenge for collaboratives is to identify the specific risk factors that must be addressed to correct or prevent the various success inhibiter problems.

Most of the risk factors that underlie success inhibiters are common to all of the inhibiters. Table 9 lists some of the success inhibiters and shows the risk factors that underlie them. This table demonstrates that some of the risk factors can apply to more than one inhibiter, and indeed, success inhibiters themselves can act as risk factors.

Preparing a table similar to Table 9 can be useful to collaboratives in planning their strategies to protect children from success inhibiters. Such a breakdown can help collaboratives to define more clearly the risk factors they should address when designing their strategies and interventions.

Establishing Baseline Conditions for Risk Factors

Chapter 4 described the need to establish baseline numbers and rates for children in communities who are not meeting the goals for being free of success inhibiters. Also needed, in addition to these baseline measurements, are estimates of

the number of children who are exposed to risk factors that can make them vulnerable to experiencing success inhibiters. This is especially critical for the children who are at the highest risk to experience success inhibiters.

To establish the baseline numbers of children exposed to specific risk factors, collaboratives should use the disaggregated data for the number of children experiencing various success inhibiters—such as juvenile delinquency, unwed teenage parenthood, or school failure—to identify the highest risk groups. For these groups, collaboratives should determine the proportion experiencing various risk factors. For example, what proportion of the girls

TABLE 9				
Relationship between Selected Risk Factors and Success Inhibiters				
	Success Inhibiters			
Risk Factor	**Child Abuse and Neglect**	**Unwed Teen Mothers**	**Delinquent Behavior**	**School Failure**
Family				
Never-married mother was a teenage mother	Yes	Yes	Yes	Yes
Mother and/or father did not complete high school	—	—	—	Yes
Mother and/or father lack parenting skills	Yes	Yes	Yes	Yes
Never-married mother heads family living in poverty	Yes		Yes	Yes
Economic	Yes	Yes	Yes	Yes
Neighborhood	Yes	Yes	Yes	Yes
Service Delivery	Yes	Yes	Yes	Yes
Individual (i.e., behavior and learning problems)	—	—	Yes	Yes
Child Abuse and Neglect	—	Yes	Yes	—
School Failure	—	Yes	Yes	—

Note: — = no relationship between risk factor and success inhibiter.

from the highest risk group of unwed teenage mothers are from poverty households? What proportion of these girls are from households headed by a never-married mother who began having children as a teenager? What proportion of the children from the highest risk group of juvenile delinquents are one or more grades behind in school? What proportion of the children from the highest risk group of those with learning and behavior disabilities were born with low birthweights? What proportion of the children from the highest risk group of those failing in school have parents who are not involved in their school activities? Table 10 provides a form for this analysis.

Other risk factor columns could be added to this table. For example, a column might be added for quantifying the number of children in the target group who are subjected to the risk factor of dysfunctional neighborhoods. The value of compiling risk factor baseline measurements for children experiencing success inhibiters is that these measurements help to validate the relationships between the risk factors and various success inhibiters. These data have the further benefit of helping

collaboratives select the risk factors that should receive priority attention.

Discussion Questions

1. What are the family conditions in the lives of children in this community that may make children susceptible to success inhibiters?

2. What are some of the deficiencies in the economic condition of families that may make some children in this community susceptible to success inhibiters?

3. What are the deficiencies in the practices, procedures, and policies of the agencies and institutions serving children and their families that may keep some children in this community from receiving the help they need to avoid success inhibiters?

4. What are the risk factors found in the social and economic environment of neighborhoods that may make some children in this community susceptible to success inhibiters?

5. What are the success inhibiters experienced by children in this community that may make them vulnerable to experiencing other success inhibiters?

	TABLE 10							
	Baseline Conditions for Risk Factors Affecting Specific Success Inhibiters, by Risk Factor and Number and Rate per 1,000 Children							
	Risk Factor							
	Mother Was Unwed Teenage Mother		Poverty Household		Parent(s) Not Active in School Life of Children		Children Behind in Grade	
Success Inhibiter	Number	Rate	Number	Rate	Number	Rate	Number	Rate
Unwed teenage motherhood								
Abuse and neglect					—	—	—	—
Juvenile delinquency								
One or more years behind in grade at ninth grade							—	—

Note: — = no relationship between risk factor and success inhibiter.

MAP 1

Distribution of Abused and Neglected Children, 1991

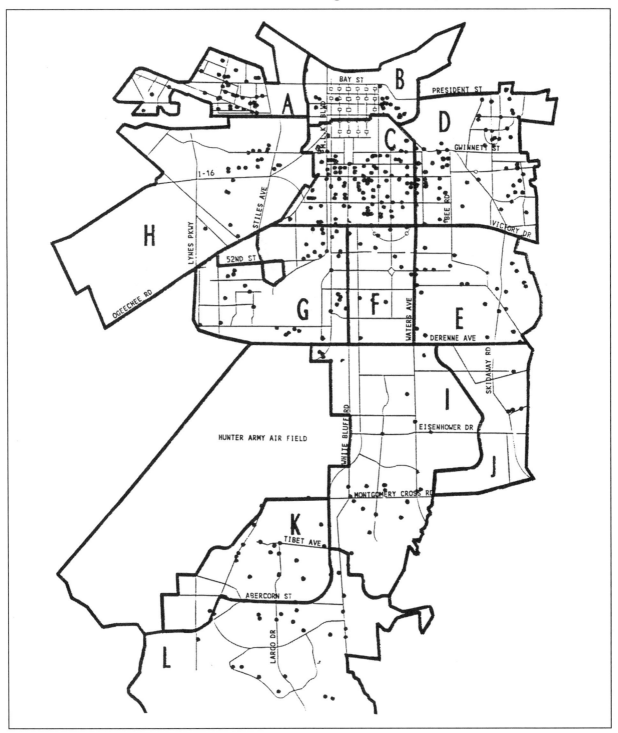

MAP 2

Distribution of Births to Unwed Teenage Girls, 1990

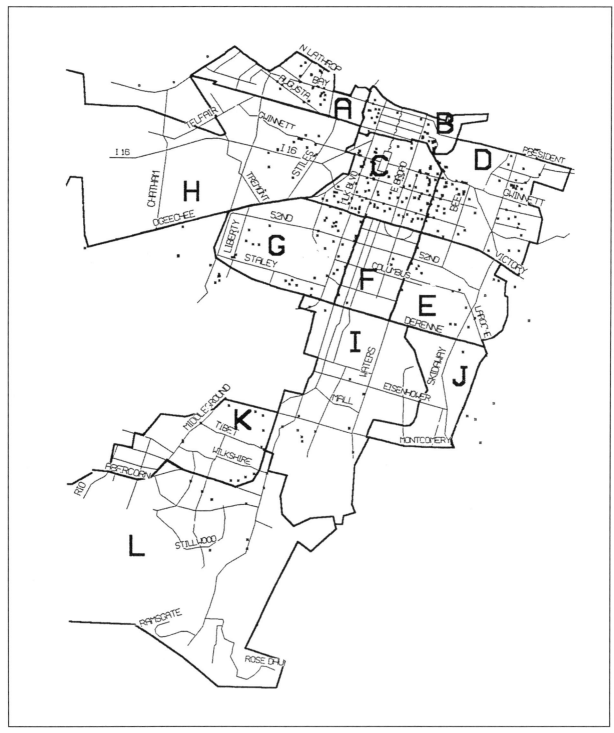

MAP 3

Distribution of Children in the Sixth Grade with the Lowest Reading Scores

MAP 4

Distribution of Aggravated Assaults in the Community, January 1, 1991 to September 13, 1991

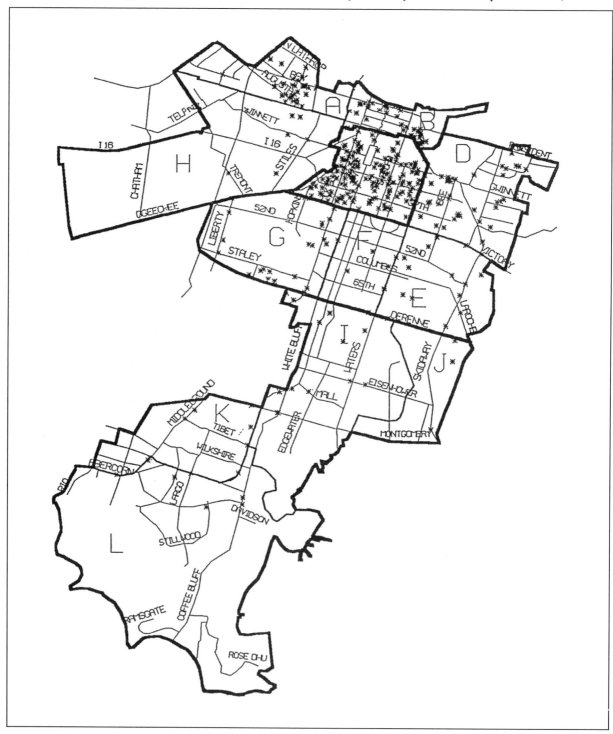

MAP 5

Distribution of Sixth-Grade Students from Female-Headed Households

MAP 6

Distribution of Substandard Housing in the Community

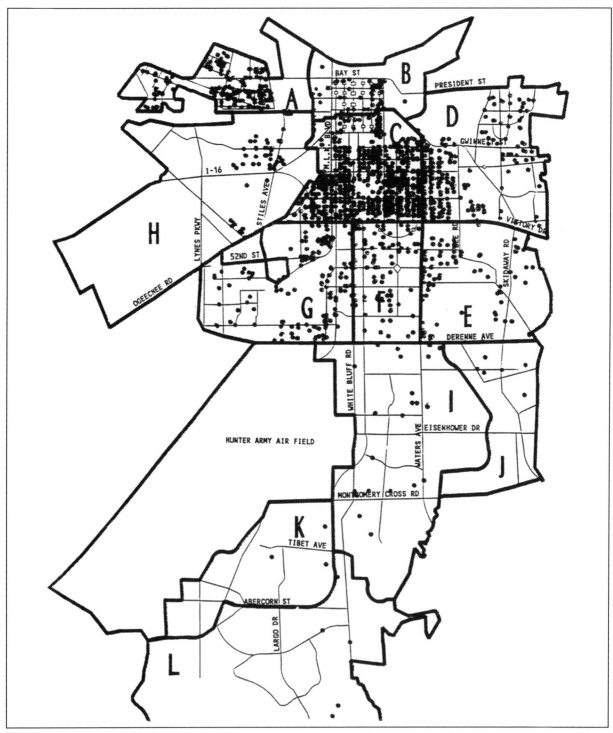

6 | 1 **Adopting Goals**
| 2 **Determining Baseline Conditions**
| 3 **Identifying Risk Factors**
| Step 4 Establishing Objectives
| 5 **Designing and Executing Strategies**
| 6 **Budgeting**
| 7 **Monitoring and Evaluating**

Once the goals have been adopted, the baseline conditions measured, and the risk factors identified, it is time to establish the objectives. *Objectives* are *specified and measurable reductions in baseline conditions and/or risk factors that the collaborative will seek to achieve by a designated time.* Objectives must address—

1. the change in the baseline conditions that is desired, and

2. the time period in which to accomplish the objectives, taking into account factors such as age and grade level of the target group selected.

Objectives are not the same as goals. *Goals* specify the ideal conditions that must exist if a collaborative's vision is to be achieved. *Objectives*, on the other hand, establish targets for reducing the rate and/or number of imperfect conditions found in the baseline measurements or risk factor analysis. They provide specific standards for determining if progress is being made in bringing the real world into conformity with the perfect world ideals expressed in the goals. For example, a perfect world *goal* might be that "all unwed teenage girls will remain free of motherhood." In the imperfect world, it might be found that the baseline birthrate for births to teenage girls is 45 per 1,000. A collaborative may decide that its *objective* will be "to reduce this rate to 30 per 1,000 within five years."[1]

Objectives are not the same as goals.

---

1. The birthrate is the number of births for each 1,000 girls in the age group for which it is quoted. In the example used, it is 45 per 1,000 girls, ages 10–19.

Relating Objectives to Baseline Measurements for Success Inhibiters

The choice of objectives should be related to the goals of the collaborative and should be established only after the baseline conditions have been measured and the risk factors have been identified. Baseline measurements for success inhibiters are the rates and numbers of children who are experiencing success inhibiters. When appropriate, as explained in Chapter 4, these numbers and rates should be disaggregated, or broken down, by race or ethnic group, gender, and age so that the highest- and lowest-risk groups can be identified. The following example illustrates the value of disaggregating the data:

> In making its baseline measurements, a collaborative finds that the total number of births to unwed teenage girls, ages 15–17, is 308, and the birthrate is 64.9 per 1,000. Without disaggregating the data, the collaborative adopts an objective that calls for this rate to be reduced to 30 per 1,000 in five years.

In this example, if the data had been disaggregated by low-risk group and high-risk group, the breakdown would show that births to the low-risk group totaled 69, and the birthrate for this group was 29 per 1,000—a rate lower than the objective that has been adopted. On the other hand, the breakdown would show that births to the high-risk group totaled 239, and the birthrate was 100.9 per 1,000 teenage girls.

On the basis of breakdown of the data in the example, it is clear that the objective to reduce the birthrate from 64.9 per 1,000 to 30 per 1,000 cannot be achieved unless the rate for the high-risk group is significantly reduced. If the rate for the low-risk group remains at or below 29 per 1,000, then the rate for the high-risk group must be reduced to at least 31 per 1,000 to achieve the objective of 30 per 1,000 teenage girls. To accomplish this objective, the number of births to the high-risk group must be reduced from 239 to 73. (This example assumes that the number of unwed teenage girls, ages 15–17, in each of the groups will not change during the five-year period. In the real world, however, these numbers will change.)

Information on the distribution by neighborhood of children experiencing success inhibiters can also be used to determine which neighborhoods should receive priority if the objective is to be achieved. This analysis will identify the neighborhoods in the community with the highest concentrations of children

who have success inhibiter problems or are at high risk to experience these problems. For example, a collaborative may find that a particular neighborhood accounts for more than 50 percent of the births to unwed teenage girls. On the basis of this finding, the collaborative determines that if the births in this neighborhood are reduced by half, the objective adopted for reducing the birthrate for unwed teenage girls will be achieved.

Assume, for example, that in a given year a community had 718 births to unwed teenage girls and that the rate for these births is 45 per 1,000. Through analysis, the community finds that 350 of these births occurred in a particular neighborhood and that the birthrate for unwed girls in this neighborhood was 87.5 per 1,000. The collaborative then determines that if this rate is cut by half, the community-wide rate would be reduced from 45 per 1,000 to 34 per 1,000. The collaborative then decides that the best way to reduce the community-wide rate is to target its strategies for reducing unwed teenage pregnancy toward this neighborhood.

Two Categories of Children to Consider

In preparing objectives for reducing success inhibiters, two categories of children must be considered: the first category is composed of those children who are already experiencing the success inhibiters. The second category takes in those children who have not yet experienced the success inhibiters.

Children Experiencing Success Inhibiters

The baseline measurements are the numbers and rates of children who, at a given point in time, are experiencing the success inhibiters addressed in the goals. For example, these baseline measurements might identify the rates and numbers of youth who did not complete high school, the rates and numbers of first births and repeat births to unwed teenage girls, or the rates and numbers of youth who have committed delinquent acts. In addition, these rates and numbers may be broken down by age, gender, and race.

For the children who are experiencing the success inhibiters, the issue is whether or not this group of children will be ignored in the efforts to help children become successful adults. If collaboratives agree that these children must be helped, then objectives must be developed for these particular children. The objectives might address reducing repeat incidents of the success inhibiter, such as reducing repeat births to unwed teenage mothers or reducing repeat incidents of juvenile delinquency, as in the following examples:

1. For repeat births: To reduce the rate of repeat births to unwed teenage mothers younger than age 20 from _____ to _____ within five years.

2. For juvenile delinquency: To reduce the recidivism rates of juvenile delinquents from _____ percent to _____ percent within five years.

For the children who are already experiencing the success inhibiters, collaboratives must also address ways to help them overcome the barriers created by the success inhibiters. For example, if teenage mothers and juvenile delinquents tend to drop out of school before graduating, then the collaboratives may wish to establish objectives for these two groups to complete school. These objectives might read as follows:

1. For teenage mothers: To increase the rate of teenage mothers completing school from _____ to _____ within five years.

2. For juvenile delinquents: To increase the rate of juvenile delinquents completing school from _____ to _____ within five years.

Children Not Yet Experiencing Success Inhibiters Who Are Vulnerable to Them

In addition to the children who are experiencing success inhibiters, there are children who have not yet experienced these inhibiters but who are vulnerable to them. For these children, objectives are needed that focus on reducing the rates at which children experience success inhibiters for the first time. For example, the baseline analysis may find that the rate of first-time births to unwed teenage girls is 47.8 per 1,000. On the basis of this finding, an objective might be adopted that calls for the rate of first-time births to unwed teenage girls to be reduced by some amount within a specified period of time. This objective might read, "To reduce the rate of first births to unwed teenage girls from 48 per 1,000 to 24 per 1,000 within five years."

Formatting the Objectives

Objectives are valuable tools in managing the execution of strategies to protect children from success inhibiters and to help mitigate or prevent risk factors that affect both children and their families. They provide specific targets to be achieved, and they place a time limit on achieving them. Once established, they provide a means of measuring the success or failure of the strategies that have been established. If progress is not being made in achieving the objectives, it may be found that the strategies are not working and need to be changed.

A format for listing objectives is suggested in Table 11. Note that the baseline rates listed in this table are the average rates for a five-year period. Also note that the objectives seek to reduce this average rate. The reason for this average is that the rates will fluctuate from year to year. Averaging smooths out fluctuations and provides a more reliable standard for measuring the success or failure of a strategy.

TABLE 11

Sample Format for Listing Objectives to Reduce Baseline Conditions for Success Inhibiters

Success Inhibiter	Goal	Baseline Condition [Average five-year rates]	Objective/Benchmark [To reduce the average five-year rate]
Unwed teenage motherhood (first-time births)	All unwed teenage girls will remain free of first-time births.	Rate for first-time births to unwed teenage mothers, ages 15–17: Low-risk rate: 18.5 per 1,000 High-risk rate: 49.2 per 1,000	For the number of first-time births to unwed teenagers, ages 15–17: Low-risk mothers: 15 per 1,000 High-risk mothers: 25 per 1,000
Unwed teenage motherhood (repeat births)	All unwed teenage mothers will remain free of further births.	Rate for repeat births to unwed teenage mothers, ages 18–19: Low-risk rate: 22.4 per 1,000 High-risk rate: 53.5 per 1,000	For the number of repeat births to unwed teenage mothers, ages 18–19: Low-risk mothers: 12 per 1,000 High-risk mothers: 30 per 1,000
School failure	All children will progress through school without being retained in any grade.	Percent of students retained in the ninth grade: 45 percent	For the percentage of students retained in the ninth grade: 25 percent

Relating Objectives to Baseline Measurements for Risk Factors

In addition to establishing objectives to reduce the rates and numbers of children experiencing success inhibiters, collaboratives may also wish to establish objectives for reducing the rates and numbers of high-risk children experiencing various risk factors that make them vulnerable to experiencing the success inhibiters. For example, in its analysis of risk factors, a collaborative may find that a high proportion of children who are failing in school are from households in which the parents do not participate in the school life of the children. On the basis of baseline measurements for this finding, a collaborative might adopt an objective to decrease the baseline number and rate of the high-risk group by some amount within a specified time.

Another example of a risk factor that a collaborative may wish to reduce in order to reduce a success inhibiter is school failure, which can be a risk factor for juvenile delinquency and for unwed teenage motherhood. This risk factor, it should be noted, is also a success inhibiter. The collaborative might adopt an objective to reduce by some amount within a specified time the rates for this risk factor among the children at high risk to become delinquents or unwed teenage mothers.

Table 12 illustrates a format for listing objectives for risk factors and presents two examples. Other examples could be selected from the benchmarks for children and families adopted by the Georgia Policy Council for Children and Families.[2] Ob-

_____

2. *Aiming for Results: A Guide to Georgia's Benchmarks for Children and Families* (Atlanta: Georgia Policy Council for Children and Families, 1996), p. 2. (See Appendix C.)

	TABLE 12	
Sample Format for Listing Objectives to Reduce Baseline Conditions for Risk Factors		
Risk Factor Underlying Success Inhibiter	**Baseline Condition for Risk Factor**	**Objective for Reducing the Baseline Condition for Risk Factor**
Risk Factor: Parents do not participate in school life of children **Success Inhibiter:** School failure	Parents of 75 percent of the children at risk do not participate in the school life of their children	Reduce the number of high-risk children whose parents are not participating in their school life from 75 percent to 40 percent within 5 years
Risk Factor: Retained in grade and overage for grade **Success Inhibiter:** Juvenile delinquency	45 percent of children at high risk to become delinquent are overage for grade and one or more years behind in grade in grade nine	Reduce the rates of these high-risk students who are overage for grade and retained in grade in the ninth grade from 45 percent to 25 percent within 5 years

jectives for reducing baseline conditions for risk factors underlying the success inhibiter, "school failure," might include the following:

1. Reduce the percentage of students at high risk to fail who are absent 10 or more days from school annually.

2. Reduce the percentage of high-risk children under age three born to unwed teenage girls living in poverty who do not receive quality early childhood development care.

3. Reduce the percentage of high-risk children that enter school with untreated vision, hearing, or health problems.

All of the risk factors addressed in Table 12 and in the preceding list reflect conditions that can make children vulnerable to experiencing success inhibiters. For each of the risk factors listed, baseline rates and numbers must first be measured as illustrated in Chapter 5, and then objectives established to reduce these baseline rates and numbers.

Reducing the rates and numbers for specific risk factors should be directly related to improving the baseline success inhibiter conditions for the target groups. Reducing the risk factor rates should be viewed as a means of achieving this end. It should not in itself be viewed as the end.

All the objectives adopted by collaboratives can be presented in formats similar to those illustrated in Tables 11 and 12. The value of these formats is that they enable collaboratives to present their objectives in a form that can be easily understood by the public. They also enable the public to understand the relationship of the objectives to the efforts of collaboratives to help children avoid or overcome success inhibiters that can keep them from becoming successful adults. In addition, they provide standards the public can use to monitor the effectiveness of the work of the collaboratives.

Discussion Questions

1. What goals have we adopted?

2. What are the baseline rates and numbers for these goals?

3. Are there differences in the rates and numbers on the basis of age, gender, and race?

4. Should our objectives address these differences?

5. Do we have baseline numbers for any of the risk factors we have identified?

6. In addition to the objectives we have adopted for reducing the rates and numbers of children experiencing success inhibiters, should we adopt objectives for reducing the rates and numbers for risk factor conditions?

7. Which of the risk factor conditions should our objectives address?

Designing and Executing Strategies

After goals have been established, baseline conditions measured, risk factors identified, and objectives adopted, the next step in the planning process is to design and execute strategies for achieving the objectives. A *strategy is defined as one or more coordinated and complementary interventions directed to helping children avoid or overcome success inhibiters.* The purpose of strategies is to reduce the number and rates of children experiencing success inhibiters. They can do this in three ways:

1. *Strategies can be directed to remove, prevent, or mitigate risk factors that are identified with specified success inhibiter problems.* This means that for children who have few, if any, of the protective supports needed to nurture, motivate, and guide them, strategies are needed that can create protective supports for them. For example, some of the children who may be vulnerable to becoming delinquents may have congenital learning and behavior problems; may live with abusive and uncaring parents; may live in a dysfunctional neighborhood; may socialize with peers with delinquency problems; and may have learning problems and physical disabilities which go untreated.

For these children, strategies are needed to address all of these conditions. These strategies must include interventions that can help the parents of the children become caring and supportive. If this cannot be accomplished, the strategies must provide the children with alternatives to their family environments. In addition, the strategies must be designed to protect these children from the negative influence of a dysfunc-

tional neighborhood and from the adverse influence of peers who are delinquents. Finally, the strategies must be directed to helping these children overcome learning and physical disability problems. All these strategies should be directed to replacing the risk factors with protective supports.

2. *Strategies can be designed to strengthen and reinforce the protective supports that children receive.* Some children who are vulnerable to success inhibiters may enjoy protective supports that can be damaged by risk factors in their lives. For these children, strategies are needed that can strengthen these protective supports by removing or mitigating risk factors. For example, some children who are at risk to become delinquent may be receiving the protective support of loving and caring parents. However, these supports may be endangered by risk factors such as poverty and unemployed or underemployed parents. These protective supports also may be damaged by neighborhood risk factors such as dysfunctional peers, neighborhood violence, and other negative neighborhood conditions. In addition, these protective supports may be weakened by a school system that is unresponsive to the parents or to the needs of the children.

In these situations, strategies must be designed that can address these factors. In this example, the strategies might seek to strengthen the protective support provided by the parents by providing job training and job placement. In addition, the strategies might seek to complement the protective support provided by the parents with interventions that create positive peer support programs in the neighborhood or that install special tutoring and remedial programs in the school system.

3. *Strategies can be designed to provide remedial interventions that can help children overcome the effects of success inhibiters.* For example, for children who are experiencing the success inhibiter of school failure, a remedial strategy might be to advance them to the proper grade by enrolling them in computer learning centers. This might be supplemented by providing these students with after-school tutors and mentors. Helping these children advance to the proper grade may keep them from experiencing other success inhibiters such as delinquency, unwed teenage motherhood, or functional illiteracy.

In each of the three approaches described above, the purpose of the strategies is to help children avoid or overcome conditions that may keep them from becoming successful adults. In the first approach, the emphasis is on building a comprehensive protective support system where one does not exist. In the second, the emphasis is on strengthening and expanding the protective supports that do exist. In the third, the emphasis is on helping children overcome the effects of the success inhibiters they are experiencing.

All three approaches address the need for protective supports. If these supports do not exist, they must be created. If they do exist but are threatened, they must be strengthened. Protective supports can be built in two ways:

1. Protective supports can be built through *remedial* interventions. If a risk factor is unemployed parents, then protective support can be built by helping parents develop job skills and find jobs. If a risk factor is parents without parenting skills, then protective support can be built by helping parents develop those skills. If a risk factor for children is being one or more grades behind in school, then protective support can be built by helping children advance to the proper grade and thereafter advance in grade without further retentions.

2. Protective support can be built through *preventive* interventions. If a risk factor is a lack of learning skills, then preventive support can be built by helping children in early childhood to develop their learning skills. If a risk factor is a dysfunctional neighborhood environment, then preventive support can be built by developing a functional neighborhood.

Strategies, then, are the *means* that will be used to accomplish desired *ends*. In this manual, the ends to be achieved are the objectives; they are the results to be achieved by means of the strategies. For example, an objective, or end, might be to reduce the number of children who are being retained in grade or who

If protective supports do not exist, they must be created.

Strategies are the means that will be used to accomplish desired ends.

are overage for grade. Such an objective might read "to reduce the over-age-for-grade rate for male students in the sixth grade from 30 percent to 15 percent within five years." A strategy, or means, to pursue this objective might be "to expand and strengthen the educational and family protective and support systems for school-age children."

Resolving Key Issues

When designing strategies and interventions, collaboratives will need to resolve the following issues:

- Which success inhibiters to address.
- Which risk factors to address.
- How to focus the strategies.
- What types of remedial and preventive interventions to use.
- How to account for intergenerational risks.
- What (and whom) to target.
- Which protective supports to strengthen.
- Which performance specifications and standards to meet.
- How to implement interventions.
- How to integrate and coordinate strategies and interventions.

Which Success Inhibiters to Address

The collaborative must decide which of the success inhibiters will be given priority. Among those that might be considered are unwed teenage pregnancy and parenthood, juvenile delinquency, school failure in the elementary grades, and abuse and neglect. In selecting its priorities, the collaborative should recognize that many of these conditions are interrelated. For example, school failure and abuse and neglect may be risk factors for unwed teenage pregnancy and parenthood. Or, being born to an unwed teenage girl may place children at risk for school failure, abuse and neglect, and juvenile delinquency. Or, school failure, behavior disabilities, and abuse and neglect can be risk factors for juvenile delinquency.

Which Risk Factors to Address

The purpose of strategies is to reduce the number and rate of children experiencing the success inhibiters. To accomplish this purpose, strategies must provide or strengthen protective supports. Strategies must be directed to removing, preventing, or mitigating risk factors in the lives of children that can lead them to experience the success inhibiters. The challenge is to design strategies that do this successfully.

For example, an objective might be to reduce the rate of births to unwed teenage girls from 45 per 1,000 to 30 per 1,000 within five years. To design a strategy to accomplish this objective, the collaborative should identify the risk factors that can place unwed teenage girls at risk to have babies. The collaborative may find that unwed teenage girls who are at the highest risk to have babies are those who are experiencing certain risk factors, such as the following:

- Being one or more grades behind in school.
- Having mothers who were unwed teenage mothers and continue to be unwed mothers.

- Having sisters who are unwed teenage mothers.
- Living in neighborhoods in which their peers are unwed teenage mothers.
- Living in neighborhoods in which a high percentage of the households consist of families headed by unwed mothers.
- Living in neighborhoods that provide no support or role models to help prevent them from becoming unwed mothers.
- Being exposed to abusive adults.
- Having no after-school supervision.

On the basis of the identified risk factors, then, what should the strategies be? What remedial strategies will help advance young girls to the proper grade level and keep them in school through high school graduation? What types of intervention strategies can be used to help families motivate and support these young girls to complete school and remain free of pregnancy and motherhood? What strategies can be used to reach into the neighborhoods in which these young girls live and help them obtain support for completing school and remaining free of motherhood? What kinds of after-school support can these children be given?

Without identification of the risk factors, the response to the objective might be to select off-the-shelf strategies that may have little or no relevance to the problems facing the children who are at risk. For example, an off-the-shelf response to reducing the rates of births to unwed teenage girls might be to provide these girls with sex education and family planning counseling. If the factors that place unwed teenage girls at risk to have babies are those listed in the above example, then these off-the-shelf interventions may be of little benefit in reducing the rates of births to unwed teenage girls.

How to Focus the Strategies

When designing strategies, a collaborative must decide what the focus of the strategies will be. One option is to make them child-focused. Another is to make them family-focused. A final option is to make them both child- and family-focused.

Research findings suggest that child-focused strategies can improve the outcomes for children but may have little or no impact on the family.[1] Such strategies include preschool, Head Start, and prekindergarten programs. Research findings also suggest that family-focused strategies may improve the performance of families but may have little impact on improving outcomes for children. Family-focused strategies that were limited primarily to home visits and parent education programs, for example, were found to show short-term benefits to the parents but had only weak effects on children.

In theory, skillfully designed and managed two-generational strategies should offer the best hope of achieving successful outcomes for children and their families. For example, for an unwed teenage mother with one child, the strategy might be directed to helping the mother complete school and learn parenting skills while at the same time helping the child develop learning skills and remain free of preventable diseases and uncorrected handicaps. As part of a two-generational strategy, interventions must be based on an analysis of both the risk factors and the protective factors at work in the lives of the children and their mothers. Such analysis might find that both remedial and preventive interventions are needed.

---

1. D. S. Gomby et al., "Long Term Outcomes of Early Childhood Programs: Analysis and Recommendations," *The Future of Children* 5, no. 3 (winter 1995): 6-24. *The Future of Children* is a series published under the auspices of the David and Lucile Packard Foundation.

What Types of Remedial and Preventive Strategies to Use

Children who are experiencing one or more success inhibiters frequently risk experiencing other success inhibiters. For these children, strategies are needed that can reduce these risks. For example, young boys who have been abused and neglected and who are one or more grades behind in elementary school may be vulnerable to becoming delinquents. To help them avoid delinquency, a collaborative may decide on strategies that can enable these boys to overcome the effects of abuse and neglect and to advance to the proper grade.

How to Account for Intergenerational Risks

Children who are themselves experiencing a success inhibiter may place their own children at risk to experience success inhibiters. A collaborative should recognize and respond to this condition when designing strategies. For example, a collaborative may target pregnant, unwed teenage girls for help. The objective may be to keep these girls in school through graduation. However, serious problems can result if the focus is only on the pregnant teenage girls. The unborn children of these girls can also be at risk to suffer a number of success inhibiting problems. They may be at risk to be born with low birthweights. Later, they may risk suffering preventable chronic illnesses, uncorrected physical and mental handicaps, abuse and neglect, and failure in school. The collaborative must be sensitive to these intergenerational conditions and design interventions to help both the pregnant teenage girls and their infants and children. A strategy to keep pregnant students in school during and after pregnancy might include the following interventions:

- Provide an alternative school for pregnant students that will remove them from what might be embarrassing relationships with their peers.

- Help pregnant students in the alternative school who are behind in grade level to advance to the proper grade.
- After the birth of their children, help unwed teenage mothers who are behind in grade level advance to the proper grade and remain in school through graduation.
- Provide child care services for teenage mothers to help them complete school.
- Provide family planning help for teenage mothers.
- Provide mentors for teenage girls during and after their pregnancies.

In addition, interventions should be provided to help the infants and children of the unwed teenage mothers. These might include the following:

- Comprehensive prenatal care for teenage girls during pregnancy.
- Intensive parenting training to teenage girls during and after their pregnancies.
- Stress management training to teenage girls during and after their pregnancies.
- A child health care program for the children of the teenage mothers.
- A neighborhood support program for the teenage mothers and their children.
- Early childhood development programs for the children of the teenage mothers.

What (and Whom) to Target

In devising strategies, a collaborative must determine what the targets of these strategies will be. These targets may be specific geographic areas within the community and the vulnerable children and their families within these areas, or they may be all the vulnerable children and their families in the community.

- *Selecting the geographic area the strategies will serve.* In most communities, children who are experiencing success inhibiters and their families often are heavily concentrated in only a few neighborhoods. When this condition exists, decisions must be made about the areas that will be targeted by the strategies. Will the target area be the entire community? Or will it be primarily those neighborhoods with the high concentrations of vulnerable children and their families?

- *Selecting the groups of children the strategies will target.* As discussed in Chapter 6, children can be grouped into two categories:

  1. *Children already experiencing success inhibiters.* The baseline conditions measure the rate and number of children who are already experiencing such success inhibiters as unwed teenage motherhood, criminal delinquency, school failure, or abuse and neglect. For these children and their families, strategies will be needed that can mitigate the effects of these success inhibiters and prevent them from occurring again.

  2. *Children who are vulnerable to success inhibiters.* The baseline measurements do not determine the number of children who are vulnerable to the success inhibiters but who have not yet experienced them. If these children are to avoid the success inhibiters and become successful adults, they must be identified, and the risk factors as well as the protective factors in their lives must be determined. Then, strategies must be designed to mitigate the risk factors and to develop or strengthen the protective support they need from their families, their neighborhoods, and the public and private service agencies and institutions serving them.

- *Determining the size of the target group.* The size of the target group must be determined or estimated. In determining the size of the group, decisions must be made about the eligibility year and eligibility requirements for those who will be served by the strategies. Will only those who meet the eligibility requirements in a specified year be included? Or, will new members be added when they meet the eligibility requirements? For example, will a target group of infants of unwed teenage mothers be limited to infants who are less than one year of age in Year One of the program, or will other infants be added whenever they are born to unwed teenage mothers? If new infants are to be added, will there be limits on the total number of infants and children who will be served in a given year? If the target group is unwed teenage mothers, will it be limited to teenage girls who are pregnant at the beginning of the start-up year, or will it consist of teenage girls who have had babies during the 12 months preceding the start-up year? Will the unwed teenage mothers in this start-up group be the only unwed teenage mothers served until they all complete high school and reach the age of twenty? Or, will new unwed teenage mothers be added each year?

Which Protective Supports to Strengthen

When designing individualized intervention plans for children, a collaborative should identify and include in these plans the protective factors that exist in the families of these children, in the neighborhoods in which these children live, and in the agencies and institutions serving these children. For example, assessment of individual children may reveal that their parents or significant relatives, such as grandmothers or aunts, are providing protective support. The assessment may also find that institutions and agencies in the target neighborhoods where the children live may have the capacity to provide protective support, but for some reason do not. This potential protective support might take the form of peer group organizations created by churches or other agencies that can support and mentor these children. Finally, assessment might identify existing community service agencies that have the skills and desire to provide protective support to children and families but do not have the necessary resources or staff. When the assessment of individual children finds that protective resources exist, the collaborative should deliberately enlist and engage the providers of these protective resources in developing intervention plans for these children.

Which Performance Specifications and Standards to Meet

A strategy consists of one or more interventions that will be directed to helping children avoid or overcome success inhibiters. For example, a delinquency prevention strategy might include interventions to address risk factors such as child abuse, school failure, peer pressure, and a dysfunctional neighborhood environment. The *interventions* to address these conditions might include early childhood development programs, Head Start, kindergarten, remedial education and tutoring, supervised after-school mentors and programs, family assistance, and neighborhood-building. Collectively, these interventions make up the strategy and are the strategy components.

After collaboratives have adopted the strategy components, they should then establish the operating specifications and performance standards for these components.

- *Operating specifications.* Operating specifications for each intervention should be established. For example, the specifications for early childhood development programs might include the types of early childhood development activities that will be provided, the skill levels these activities will be expected to produce, the qualifications that will be required of the staff, and the ratio of children to staff.

- *Performance standards.* Performance standards should be established for each intervention. These standards should prescribe performance criteria for the intervention. These criteria might specify the frequency with which the service is to be provided to clients, the level of parent participation that will be sought, and the level of continuing support that will be provided to the children being served and their families.

How to Implement Interventions

To carry out interventions, implementation procedures must be established. These procedures are called administrative components and include the following:

- *Methods for entering members of the target group into the interventions.* Clients can enter the interventions in three ways: by self-admission, by the outreach efforts of the intervention agencies or collaborative, or by referrals from collaborating agencies and individuals.

  1. *Self-Admission.* Of these three ways, the self-admission procedure may be the least effective in reaching the target groups. Individuals who will take the initiative to admit themselves to an intervention usually represent only a small proportion of those who need to be reached.

  2. *Outreach.* Outreach programs are used to ensure that all members of the target group who need the services of the intervention are contacted and helped to enter the intervention. Without an outreach program, many of those in the target group who need help will not be reached. They will not admit themselves, and they may not be referred; if referred, they may not follow through. In addition to reaching out to those who need help, an outreach program also provides an opportunity for the outreach staff to assess the

household and neighborhood environments of the individuals and families whom the intervention is intended to serve. If an outreach program is to bring clients into the intervention, then a set of procedures must be designed for this program.

3. *Referrals*. A referral procedure can be established to bring members of the target group into the intervention. Under this procedure, service agencies and institutions refer clients to the intervention on the basis of an assessment of their needs. To be effective in reaching the members of the target group, all the agencies and organizations in contact with these members must participate in a formal referral system. In addition, the referral system should establish follow-up procedures to help ensure that referred clients enter the interventions and receive the services they need.

Contact with the members of the target group should not be left to chance and circumstance. A formal contact procedure should be established. This procedure should establish policies for self-admissions, outreach, and referrals. In addition, this procedure should specify the linkages that will exist among the three methods.

• *Intake procedures for the target group.* An intake procedure will be needed to enter clients into the interventions. If clients must be served by several interventions, each operated by a different agency, the intake procedure must address the following questions:

Will there be a central intake process, or will each agency have its own intake system?

If each agency is to have an intake system, will the intake information collected by each agency be shared with the other agencies?

Under a decentralized intake arrangement, how will the intake activities of the different agencies be coordinated and controlled to ensure delivery of a complementary continuum of interventions to the clients?

• *Client assessment.* If the clients who enter the interventions are to be assessed, then procedures for making these assessments must be established. When developing these procedures, the collaborative should address these questions:

Will there be a central assessment unit staffed by skilled and trained assessors, or will the intervention agencies do the assessments?

What will be assessed?

What will be the specifications for making assessments?

How will the assessments be used?

What should be the qualifications of the assessors?

Who should participate in the assessments?

• *Intervention plans.* Each client from the target group who will be served by the strategies will need an intervention plan based on an assessment of the client. This plan should establish objectives for the interventions, such as keeping a pregnant student in school, advancing to grade a student who is behind in grade, helping an unwed mother avoid further pregnancies, preventing first-time pregnancy in an unwed teenage girl, or correcting and preventing violent behavior in a youth. The interventions should be directed to removing or mitigating the applicable risk factors and strengthening the protective factors that have been found so that the objectives specified in the intervention plan can be achieved. Ideally, the plan should be formal and comprehensive rather than informal and piecemeal. It should be designed jointly by the client and a skilled and trained intervention specialist.

- *Management of intervention plans.* Intervention plans for clients must be carried out and a procedure established to help ensure that this happens. This procedure might be a system under which case managers are given responsibility for managing the execution of the plans. Under such a system, case managers are responsible for monitoring to ensure that the interventions are provided to clients in the manner prescribed in the plans. Further, case managers work to ensure that the clients follow the prescriptions set forth in their intervention plans. Case managers also evaluate the results to determine if the objectives specified in the intervention plans have been achieved. Finally, if the interventions did not work, the case managers report this to the parties responsible for prescribing the interventions.

How to Integrate and Coordinate Strategies and Interventions

A factor that negatively affects the outcomes for children at risk is the fragmented, uncoordinated, and categorical delivery of services to children and their families. In designing strategies and interventions to help children, a system is needed for integrating and coordinating services. Among other issues to consider, this system should address creation of the following:

- Integrated outreach and referral procedures.
- Centralized intake and assessment system.
- Consolidated information system.
- System for coordinating referrals for interventions and for follow-up.
- Integrated case management system.
- Co-location system for intervention services.
- Consolidated budget procedure for the interventions.

Calculating the Cost of the Strategy Plans

When developing the strategy plans, the cost of implementing interventions specified in the plans should be calculated. Included in these calculations should be costs for such elements as the following:

1. The intake system.
2. The assessment system.
3. The client identification and contact system.
4. The case management system.
5. The interventions; for example,
   - parenting classes,
   - remedial education,
   - family counseling, and
   - neighborhood organizing.

From these calculations, a multiyear cost plan should be developed by fiscal year and made a part of the strategy plan. This plan should list by amount both the costs and the sources of funds that will be used to pay these costs. An example of a format for a multiyear cost plan is shown in Table 13. (Also see Chapter 8 on budgeting.)

Cost plans should be updated annually. The current year of the cost plan should be the basis for the current year's budget. After it becomes the budget, the current year should be dropped from the cost plan and the plan extended forward one year. This will ensure that a five-year cost plan is always available. This plan can be used to prepare the annual budget for implementing and managing the strategy plan. In addition, it can be used to project the amount of income that will be needed for the plan in the future.

TABLE 13					
Format for a Multiyear Cost Plan to Support Strategy Plans					
	Cost Allocations				
Strategies	Year 1	Year 2	Year 3	Year 4	Year 5
Intervention					
1. Parenting classes					
2. Remedial education					
3. Targeted family counseling					
4. Neighborhood organizing					
Administrative Component					
1. Intake system					
2. Assessment system					
3. Outreach system					
4. Case management system					
Source of Revenue					
1. Grants from the state					
2. Local government contributions					
3. Private contributions					
4. Foundation grants					
5. In-kind services					
6. Other					
Totals					

Executing the Strategies

After the strategies to accomplish the objectives have been selected, a plan must be developed for executing them. The purpose of this execution plan should be to ensure that the interventions specified in the strategies begin on time and that they complement and reinforce one another. This plan must also seek to ensure that the agencies responsible for performing the strategies will be accountable for achieving results.

Designing the execution plan will not be easy. It must address matters such as management, interagency agreements, creation of intervention services, coordination and control, collaboration, budget development, establishing a timetable, and data collection.

Management

Effective implementation of a strategy plan cannot be accomplished without proper management. A manager's position should be created, and the duties established for this position should include the following:

1. Being responsible for directing and guiding the development, negotiation, and monitoring of contracts with agencies that will provide the intervention services.

2. Being responsible for organizing and directing intervention services, if any, that will be provided by the collaborative organization.

3. Being responsible for ensuring that necessary and appropriate coordination of the work of the various agencies occurs and that the performance and effectiveness of the interventions provided by these agencies are evaluated on a regular basis.

4. Being responsible for directing the preparation and monitoring of the budget for implementing the plan to ensure that spending stays within budgetary limits and that revenue collections meet revenue estimates.

5. Being responsible for reporting to the collaborative on a regular basis regarding the status and progress of the plan's implementation and performance.

Interagency Agreements

Many of the interventions specified in the strategy plan can be provided by local public and nonprofit agencies. For example, the plan may call for prenatal care to be provided to pregnant teenage girls. The local health department is a prenatal care provider. For this intervention, then, the health department would be solicited to provide this service to the target group.

In this case and in other cases where independent agencies are solicited to provide intervention services, a means must be found to hold these agencies responsible and accountable for performance. If the collaborative has the funds and authority to contract for intervention services, then accountability can be obtained under the provisions of a contract. This contract should specify what is expected of the agencies delivering the interventions, the means that will be used to hold them accountable for performance, and the penalties that will be imposed for noncompliance. This contract should also specify the performance standards that the agencies will be required to meet and the results that will be expected from the interventions they will provide.

For example, the objective might be to prevent pregnant students from dropping out of school, both during their pregnancies and after their babies are delivered. A related objective might be to ensure that after delivery of their babies, these students will remain free of repeat pregnancies. The contract to provide the services to accomplish these objectives should define the procedures that will be used to identify and reach the pregnant students and should specify the interventions the agency will use to keep the pregnant students in school. The contract should also specify the interventions that will be used to help keep the students free of further pregnancies.

A collaborative may also contract with independent agencies to implement strategies under a no-fee agreement. Under this arrangement, the agencies agree to pay the full cost of implementing the strategies from their own funds. Compliance with the contract depends on the good will of the agencies providing the interventions. If such agreements are a part of a community collaborative arrangement, there should not be an enforcement problem. However, if the agencies only give lip service to the agreements and make no real effort to collaborate, then enforcement of the contracts can become a problem. In such cases, financial incentives or penalties cannot be used. Further, it is unlikely that legal action can be taken. In such cases, the collaborative may elect to use the power of public opinion to bring about compliance with contractual commitments.

Creation of Intervention Services

When the intervention services called for by the plan are not available in the community, these services must be created and an agency must be selected to provide them. For example, the plan may call for pregnant teenagers and new teenage mothers to receive intensive and comprehensive parenting training, but training is not available from any of the agencies in the community. For this intervention, a parenting training program must be designed and an agency selected to administer it. The agency might be the collaborative itself or an existing agency that provides related services.

Coordination and Control

Usually more than one agency will be needed to provide the interventions called for in the strategy plan. The work of these agencies must be coordinated and controlled to ensure that they provide a continuum of complementary interventions. For example, the strategies adopted to keep pregnant, unwed teenage girls in school and to achieve successful outcomes for their children may call for interventions to be provided by the health department, the school system, local governments, and the local Department of Family and Children Services.

The collaborative must adopt procedures for integrating the work of each of these agencies into a system of coordinated and complementary services. Issues that should be addressed include client intake procedures,

Usually more than one agency will be needed to provide the interventions.

client assessment procedures, and client contact procedures. Other issues to be addressed are the client loads each agency will have, the performance standards expected from each agency, and the information to be supplied on a specified schedule by the agency.

Collaboration

A plan designed for coordinating and controlling the work of the agencies must address the critical issue of collaboration. For a continuum of complementary interventions to be accomplished, the agencies involved must collaborate. From the start, they must be active participants in developing the strategy plan. They must agree with the goals and objectives and be active participants in efforts to identify the risk factors to be addressed. Finally, they must be active participants in designing and selecting the interventions.

Although the choice of interventions should not be imposed on them by the strategy plan, agencies should not design and implement their own interventions without the review and approval of the collaborative body. Interventions designed by the agencies should be required to meet the criteria established by the collaborative for addressing risk factors, performance standards, and objectives. Without this coordination and control, fragmented and uncontrolled responses to problems are likely, and the results sought for children and their families may not be achieved.

Budget Development

Once the strategy plan has been adopted, the next step is to adopt a budget for the first implementation year. This budget will establish the program of work for this first year, allocate funds to pay for this program of work, and identify the sources of funds to cover these allocations. Each year thereafter, a new budget will be needed. Each of these new budgets should be based on the multiyear cost plan. Chapter 8 describes budgeting in more detail and presents a sample budget.

The Timetable

The fiscal year, or budget year, for implementing strategies may begin on January 1 and end on December 31. However, in the start-up year the interventions called for in the strategies may not be fully in place for several months. This can mean that such recurring costs as travel, rents, utilities, and salaries and benefits will be lower in the first year than they will be in subsequent years. On the other hand, nonrecurring start-up costs such as expenditures for furniture and equipment usually will be higher in the start-up year than they will be in subsequent years. Delays in making the new program fully operational in the start-up year can also mean that the number of clients that can be served in this year will be lower than it will be in future years. This will affect the amount of progress that can be made in the first year toward achieving the objectives. To avoid misunderstanding and confusion because of necessary start-up delays and to avoid budgetary problems, a timetable for implementing the interventions should be established. An example of such a timetable appears in Table 14.

Data Collection

An information system is needed to manage the interventions specified in the strategy plan. This system should be developed and administered by trained management information staff. The information system should include the following:

1. Baseline data for each of the goals, broken down into appropriate categories.

2. Data for each client, including a listing of the risk factors affecting that client and the protection and support the client is receiving.

TABLE 14		
Timetable for Implementing the Strategies		
Action to Be Taken	**Responsible Party**	**Date to Be Completed**

1. Create an organization to administer the program
    a. Appoint staff
    b. Organize and equip office
    c. Develop and adopt operating procedures
    d. Train staff
    e. Etc.		

2. Draft procedures for intake and assessment of clients to be served by the interventions		
3. Train intake and assessment personnel		
4. Negotiate contracts for those strategy interventions that will be provided under a contract		
5. Begin accepting clients into the intervention programs		

3. A list of the objectives established for each client and the interventions that have been prescribed to achieve them.

4. Reports describing the progress being made in achieving the objectives adopted for both the clients and the strategy plan.

The data system must have the capacity to aggregate the data in a form that will permit collaboratives to determine whether or not efforts to improve the baseline conditions are succeeding. Aggregated data should be provided for such conditions as infant mortality rates, teenage parenthood and pregnancy rates, and school retention rates. This data should be broken down by age, race, gender, or other categories as required for planning and managing the strategies.

Formatting the Strategies

The preceding sections have outlined the issues that must be addressed in developing a strategy plan. Tables 15, 16, and 17 provide examples of how a strategy plan might look. In these tables, the goals for the plan are listed first; then, the details of the plan are summarized. Table 18 summarizes the strategies, management issues, costs, and the outcomes expected.

Discussion Questions

1. What is the purpose of strategies and how can they be used to accomplish this purpose?

2. Which of the success inhibiters will our strategies target?

3. What objectives will the strategies pursue?

4. What are the risk factors that the strategies will address?

5. What will be the focus of our strategies? Will they be child-focused? family-focused? both?

6. Will our strategies be remedial or preventive? Or will they be a combination of both?

7. Do our strategies take into consideration intergenerational risks? What are these risks, and who can they affect?

8. Which groups will the strategies target?

9. Do our strategies address the need to strengthen protective supports that are being weakened by risk factors?

10. What are the components or interventions that make up our strategy and what are the performance standards for these interventions?

11. How will the interventions be made available to clients? How will these clients be brought into the interventions?

12. What will be the cost of executing the strategies? Do we have a five-year cost plan?

13. How will the cost of the plan be funded?

14. Do we have a schedule for implementing the strategy plans?

15. How will the execution of the plans be managed?

16. Will the collaborative use interagency agreements and contracts to carry out the strategy plans?

17. Will the collaborative operate any of the interventions?

18. How will the work of the various agencies providing the interventions be coordinated and controlled?

TABLE 15

Plan Summary for Unwed Teenage Girls

Goals	Baseline Conditions	Risk Factors	Objectives	Strategies	Administrative Components
All unwed teenage girls will remain free of pregnancy and parenthood.	Rate for first-time births to unwed teenage girls ages: 15–17: 32 per 1,000 18–19: 45 per 1,000	Failing in school and one or more years behind in grade. A mother who was an unwed teenage mother. Sexual abuse as a child. Peer groups in the neighborhood. No knowledge of the costs, burdens, and responsibilities of being a teenage parent. Other.	Within five years, reduce birthrates for first-time births to unwed teenage girls ages: 15–17: 20 per 1,000 18–19: 25 per 1,000	Provide sanctions (when indicated), counseling, and stress management training to families with records of abuse to children. Provide instructions to children on the obstacles to success that early parenthood will create for them and their children. Beginning in the third grade, provide alternative instruction to children who are failing or are behind in grade, and continue to monitor their school performance and intervene as required. Provide after-school programs to protect the girls from adverse influence by their peers.	Conduct an early identification program for children in school who are at risk to become teenage parents because of their family environment, neighborhood environment, and school performance. Assess the children, their families, and their neighborhoods to identify risk factors that must be addressed, and develop with the children and their families a plan to help them overcome these risk factors. Assign a case manager to the children and their families to ensure that the help specified in the plan is provided by the responsible agency and that the children and families use the help that is available. This help may include the following: • family counseling • parenting training • alternative school instruction • sanctions against abuse • family responsibility instruction • neighborhood interventions • after-school programs • in-school interventions Report regularly on the performance of the agencies and the results being achieved for the children and families.

TABLE 16

Plan Summary for Pregnant, Unwed Teenage Girls and Unwed Teenage Mothers

Goals	Baseline Conditions	Risk Factors	Objectives	Strategies	Administrative Components
All pregnant, unwed teenage girls and unwed teenage parents will remain free of repeat births and will complete school.	Rate for repeat births to unwed teenage mothers ages: 15–17: 10 per 1,000 18–19: 37 per 1,000 Retention rate in ninth grade for female students: 32 percent Drop-out rates for female students who were in the ninth grade but did not reach twelfth grade: 27 percent	*For repeat births* Lack of family planning guidance and assistance. Peer pressure. Lack of family support. Lack of school success. *For retained in grade* Course failure and grade retention beginning in elementary school. Lack of family support and assistance. Lack of recognition by school that special assistance in mastering material is needed. Lack of role models and mentors. Lack of neighborhood support. *For dropping out of school* Pregnancy and parenthood while a student. Unaffordable child care for teenage parents. School failure. Lack of family support. Lack of understanding by teenage girls that dropping out of school will create barriers to becoming successful adults and parents.	*For repeat births* Within five years, reduce birthrate for repeat births to unwed teenage girls ages: 15–17: 5 per 1,000 18–19: 20 per 1,000 *For retained in grade* Within five years, reduce the retention rate for female students in the ninth grade to 20 percent or less. *For dropping out of school* Within five years, reduce the drop-out rate for female students to 15 percent or less.	*For repeat births* Provide family planning assistance and guidance to unwed teenage girls with one or more children. Provide counseling on the problems that additional births can create for the children and the mothers. Provide mentoring and peer assistance directed to helping unwed teenage mothers avoid repeat births. *For retained in grade* Provide alternative instruction to advance to the proper grade level female students who have been retained, beginning at the lowest grade level at which retention occurs. Provide parenting training and counseling to the family of the female student at risk to be retained. Help the female students avoid pregnancy and parenthood. *For dropping out of school* Provide child care for the children of the unwed teenage mothers so they can complete school.	With the help of the health department, the school system, and the Department of Family and Children Services, identify unwed teenage girls with one or more children who are in school and who live in the target area. Develop a success plan with each of the mothers for themselves and their children. Assign teenage mothers and their children to a case manager. The case manager's responsibilities will be to help ensure that the appropriate agencies provide the help required of them and that the young mothers and their children use this help as specified in their success plan. This help may include the following: • family planning • remedial education • mentoring • health care • family counseling • parenting training • job training and job placement • day care for the children Specify in the plan the help that is needed and success objectives to be achieved. Sign contracts with the agencies that will be responsible for providing the intervention help. Designate a lead agency to coordinate the interventions.

TABLE 17

Plan Summary for Children Born to Unwed Teenage Mothers

Goals	Baseline Conditions	Risk Factors	Objectives (reduce within five years)	Strategies	Administrative Components
All infants born to unwed teenage girls will be born with normal birthweights, will be free of preventable congenital diseases, and will survive birth and the first year of life. All children ages –6 years old born to teenage girls will survive early childhood and will be free of preventable diseases and correctable handicaps. All children born to teenage girls will enter school ready to learn, will not be retained in the first three grades, and will be grade-level proficient in reading, math, and language skills on entering the fourth grade. All children born to teenage girls will remain free of child abuse and neglect.	Infant mortality rate for babies born to teenage girls: ? Low birthweight for babies born to teenage girls: ? Morbidity rates for children ages 1–6 years old born to unwed teenage girls for preventable diseases and correctable disabilities: ? Abuse and neglect rates for children ages 1-6 years old born to unwed teenage girls: ? Failure rates in the fourth grade for children born to unwed teenage girls: ?	*For infant mortality, low birthweight, and congenital diseases* Spacing too short between pregnancies. Poor nutrition. Mother passes congenital conditions, such as venereal diseases, to unborn child. Mother passes drug dependency to unborn child. *For morbidity rates for preventable diseases and correctable handicaps* Teenage mothers lack skills and knowledge to be attentive to the health care needs of their children, such as: • immunizations • correctable handicaps • regular health checks and care Health care facilities are not conveniently accessible. *For abuse and neglect* Teenage mothers cannot manage stress and cannot provide protective support. *For school success* Teenage mothers do not have skills to prepare their children for entering school.	*Infant mortality* rates for infants born to unwed teenage mothers to: ? *Low birthweight* rates for infants born to unwed teenage mothers to: ? *Congenital disease* rates for infants born to unwed teenage mothers to: ? *Morbidity* rates for preventable diseases and correctable handicaps to: ? *Abuse and neglect* rates for children born to unwed teenage mothers to: ? *School retention* rates in the fourth grade for children born to unwed teenage mothers to: ?	*For infant mortality, low birthweight, and congenital diseases,* provide family planning assistance to unwed teenage girls who are pregnant and/or who have children to prevent further pregnancies and spacing between pregnancies that is too short. Address nutritional needs during pregnancy. Treat conditions in pregnant teenage girls that can lead to their children acquiring a congenital condition and/or drug dependency. *For morbidity rates,* provide immunizations to the children of unwed teenage girls and provide examinations to identify and remedy correctable handicaps. *For school success,* place the children born to unwed teenage girls in preschool programs and kindergarten. *For all risk factors, including abuse and neglect,* provide parenting training to expectant teenage girls and to teenage mothers, including: • child health care • house management • stress management • child development • using service agencies • financial management Provide child development services to the children born to unwed teenage girls.	Identify unwed teenage mothers with children and pregnant, unwed teenage girls through the schools, the health department, and other means. Assess and develop success plans with them and for them and their born and unborn children. Assign the unwed teenage mothers and their children or the pregnant mother to a case manager. Identify target area: e.g., neighborhood "c." Identify target group, such as: • pregnant, unwed teenage students • unwed teenage mothers in school and in area "c" • children ages 1–10 years old who were born to unwed teenage girls

		TABLE 18					
		Implementation Summary					
Strategies	Target Groups	Number	Lead Agency	Responsible Agency	Budget	Expected Outcomes
---	---	---	---	---	---	---
Family planning services	Unwed teenage girls who are pregnant and/or teenage girls with children.	300	Collaborative	Health Department	$ 40,000	Reduced repeat pregnancies.
Prenatal care	Unwed, pregnant teenage girls who are in school or who live in area "c."	450	Collaborative	Health Department	$ 90,000	Reduced infant mortality rates and low birthweight rates.
Alternative school	Unwed teenage girls who are pregnant and/or have children.	300	Collaborative	School system	$150,000	Teenage girls remained in school while pregnant.
Alternative instruction	Unwed teenage girls grades 3 through 8 who are one or more grades behind in school.	450	Collaborative	School system	$450,000	Reduced retention rates for female students in ninth grade.
Parenting training Stress management training	Unwed teenage girls who are pregnant and/or are parents.	450 girls who are either in or out of school and who are living in area "c."	Collaborative	Health Department School system Collaborative Other	$ 60,000	Reduced incidence of abuse and neglect. Reduced incidence of poor health. Reduced retentions in the first grade.
Child health care Immunizations Disability remediation	Newborns and older children of unwed teenage mothers.	450	Collaborative	Health Department	$ 90,000	Reduced early childhood deaths. Reduced morbidity rates for preventable diseases and correctable disabilities.
Day care Preschool program	Newborns and older children of unwed teenage mothers still in school. Children 3–4 years old of unwed teenage mothers.	250	Collaborative	Public and private day care agencies	$250,000	Reduced numbers of teenage mothers who dropped out of school. Reduced retentions in the first grade.
Pre-Kindergarten	5-year-old children of unwed teenage mothers.	150	Collaborative	School system	$200,000	Reduced retentions in grades 1 through 4.

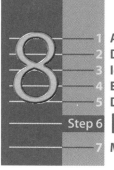

Step 6 Budgeting

Once the strategy plan has been approved, an annual program of work to implement this plan must be adopted; the costs of this work must be calculated; and the money must be found and appropriated to cover these costs. The process by which this is done is called *budgeting*. This chapter defines a budget, presents a budget outline, and describes and illustrates the parts of a budget.

The budget model presented in this chapter is a program-performance, outcome-based budget. A budget developed using this model presents workload information, establishes performance standards for the work elements, and presents the outcome objectives for the work programs. This model differs from the line-item model and the program budget model. A line-item budget usually appropriates money to expense items rather than to programs and does not address workloads, performance standards, or outcome objectives. A program budget usually appropriates money to programs but does not specify workloads, performance standards, or outcome objectives.[1]

What Is a Budget?

A budget is a plan for funding the annual work programs. For a collaborative, the work program will consist of the interventions specified in the strategy plan. A collaborative's budget that conforms to the program-performance, outcome-based budget model will describe the interventions that will be provided, the performance standards established for these services, and the objectives for these interventions. It will allocate funds to pay the costs for each intervention and will list, by source and amount, the money and other resources that will be used to pay these costs.

The parts of a budget. A budget has four parts:

Part One. The budget message should summarize the programs of work proposed for the budget year, the objectives to be achieved, the costs of the work programs, and the revenue plan to fund the costs.

Part Two. The funding plan should show by source the amount of money and in-kind contributions and services the organization expects to receive for the budget year to pay for the work programs.

Part Three. This part of the budget should list the work programs that will be carried out and the amount of funds and equivalent resources that will be allocated to each program. It should also present a breakdown of the various items of cost, the personnel positions authorized for each work program, and the number of employees in each position.

Part Four. This section of the budget should list each work program and the workloads, performance standards, and objectives established for the programs. When possible, this section should also list the cost of performing

---

1. The budget model described in this chapter is one that is used by many local governments. It is valued because it provides policy makers and the public with information that links costs and tax levies to workloads, performance expectations, and results objectives. However, this model may differ from the models specified by agencies or foundations that provide grants.

each work unit and/or the cost of serving each consumer.

A simple program-performance, outcome-based budget is illustrated below. The first part is the budget message. The second part shows the amount of funds, by source, projected to be available in the budget year. How these funds will be allocated for the work programs is shown in the third part. The fourth part details one of the work programs (see page 72). Note that this budget is balanced, so that money projected to be received during the year equals the total allocations.

The budget illustrated under part III, "Allocations for the Intervention Programs," is a program budget. This means that lump

---

Collaborative for Children and Families
Somewhere, Georgia
Budget for 199 _____

I. Budget Message

A. Description of the intervention programs that will be carried for the budget period and the objectives of these programs.

B. Summary of the allocations to cover the cost of each intervention program.

C. Summary, by source, of the amount of money and the dollar equivalent of other resources that will be used to fund these allocations.

II. Projected Income for the Budget Year

Source	Estimated Amount
Funds from the City of Somewhere	$ 40,000
Funds from the County of Somewhere	$ 40,000
Funds from the state	$100,000
Contributions from the public and in-kind services	$ 29,150
Total	
	$209,150

III. Allocations for the Intervention Programs

Program/Intervention	Appropriation
1. After-school program for delinquency prevention	$ 89,150
2. Teenage pregnancy prevention program	$ 85,000
3. Literacy improvement/reading and math tutoring program	$ 25,000
4. State-of-children report	$ 10,000
Total	$209,150

sum allocations, or appropriations, are made to each of the programs that will be operated during the budget year. These allocations are made to pay for personnel, equipment, supplies, and other resources needed for the program.

The budget should also show, in summary form, the allocations for each of the expenditure categories to pay for operating resources. The breakdown shown below for one of the work programs—the "After-School Program for Delinquency Prevention"—illustrates how this can be done. Also shown is a schedule of the personnel positions that will be needed for the program and their respective salaries.

A similar breakdown can be made for each of the other interventions listed under "Allocations for the Intervention Programs."

Each of the expenditure classifications listed consists of several cost items. These must be identified and their costs calculated using work sheets, such as that shown below for staff positions. For each major expenditure, the items of cost that will be covered are listed.

Salaries and benefits: Included in this expenditure category are the cost of salaries, the cost of social security, and the cost of life and health insurance, if any, for each position.

After-School Program for Delinquency Prevention
Allocations for Resource Categories

Expenditure Category	Allocation
1. Salaries and benefits	$68,250
2. Contractual services	$11,500
3. Other costs	$ 6,400
4. Equipment	$ 3,000
Total	$89,150

Personnel Schedule

Position	Salary
1. Professional position	$34,000
2. Assistant	$25,500

Staff Position	Annual Salary	Social Security	Life and Health Insurance	Total
Professional position	$34,000	$2,250	$2,500	$38,750
Assistant's position	$25,500	$1,500	$2,500	$29,500
Total	$59,500	$3,750	$5,000	$68,250

Contractual services: Examples of contractual services are travel, insurance, utilities, consultants, and services of a similar nature.

Contractual Service	Allocation
Telephone	$ 1,300
Electricity	$ 2,700
Other utilities	$ 1,000
Consultant contract	$ 2,500
Professional services such as auditor and legal services	$ 1,000
Contracts with other agencies	$ 3,000
Total	$11,500

Other costs: Examples of "other costs" are supplies, printing, postage, travel, and similar costs.

Other Cost	Allocation
Paper	$ 700
File folders and related materials	$ 300
Pens, pencils, paper clips, etc.	$ 200
Printing materials and supplies	$ 500
Postage	$1,200
Travel	$3,000
Miscellaneous	$ 500
Total	$6,400

Equipment: Equipment includes items such as office furniture, calculators, typewriters, file cabinets, and computers. (In some cases, the cost of equipment cannot be paid from grant funds. In such cases, these costs can be covered either by in-kind contributions or by funds other than grant funds. Regardless of how they are paid for, all costs should be included in the budget, and the means used to pay for them should be identified in the revenues section of the budget.)

Equipment	Allocation
Desk and chair	$ 900
File cabinets	$ 300
Word processor	$1,800
Total	$3,000

The fourth part of a budget is the summary of the work to be accomplished for each intervention component. The example below shows how this might be presented. In the example, the goal is presented, both the target area and target group are identified, the baseline conditions are presented, and the objectives are listed. The interventions that will be used and the workloads for each intervention are then presented.

IV. The Work Program: After-School Program for Delinquency Prevention

Goal:	All boys will remain free of delinquency.
Target area:	Area "C"
Target group:	Boys ages 10–17.
Baseline conditions:	Two hundred boys between the ages of 10 and 17 years old in Area "C" have a delinquency record. This is 10 percent of the boys in this age group who live in the neighborhood. Of the 200 boys with delinquency records, 100 have two or more convictions.
Objectives:	To reduce the repeat convictions from 50 percent to 25 percent. To reduce first-time convictions by 50 percent.

Intervention	Cost Allocation	Workload in Participants Served	Cost per Participant
Assign juveniles with one or more convictions to mentors	$ 9,150	200 boys	$ 45.75/boy
Provide remedial reading and math tutoring for convicted juveniles who are one or more grades behind in school	$20,000	100 boys	$200.00/boy
Provide supervised recreation for all at-risk boys in Area "C"	$40,000	500 boys	$ 80.00/boy
Establish a parent involvement program for the parents of all the at-risk boys	$20,000	300 parents	$66.66/parent
Totals	$89,150	1,100 participants	$81.05 per participant

Complying with the Budget

Ensuring compliance with budget allocations can be accomplished in three ways:

1. *By prohibiting expenditures for intervention programs from exceeding their allocations.* Compliance with the allocations for each intervention program can be accomplished by prohibiting expenditures that exceed the allocations for each intervention program. When all of the funds allocated for a program have been spent, then no more costs should be incurred until additional funds are authorized. This authorization is granted by formally amending the budget to increase the allocation for the program. Procedures for making formal budget adjustments should be a part of the budget management policies adopted by a collaborative.

2. *By prohibiting spending for major expenditure categories from exceeding their allocations.* Compliance for major expenditure categories such as personal services or contractual services can be controlled by prohibiting spending for an expenditure category from exceeding the allocation for it. For example,

if $68,000 is allocated to pay personal services costs, spending for this cost category should not exceed this amount. However, to permit program managers greater flexibility, the budget policies could authorize them to make transfers of funds from the allocations of one expenditure category to another. For example, a manager may find that the allocation for personal services will not be adequate but that the expenditures for equip-

Procedures for making formal budget adjustments should be part of budget management policies.

ment will be lower than the amount allocated for this purpose. Under these circumstances, the manager could be given authority under the budget policies of the collaborative to decrease the amount of the allocation for equipment and increase the amount of the allocation for personal services. A record of these transactions should be maintained and a report of these transactions should be made to the collaborative.

3. *By prohibiting spending for minor line-item expenditures from exceeding their allocations.* For minor line-item expenditures, such as paper supplies or telephone costs, compliance can be accomplished by prohibiting the spending for each of these line items from exceeding their allocations. This line-item budget control is more costly to administer than the first two methods. Further, the benefits gained do not justify the cost. Under most circumstances, a manager should be permitted to overspend for minor line items as long as the total expenditures for minor line items in a major expenditure category do not exceed the total allocation.

For example, the work sheet for "other costs" (page 72) shows travel cost at $3,000 and postage cost at $1,200. In the course of the budget year, it may be found that another $500 will be needed for postage. The manager should be able to obtain this $500 by reducing the travel cost item to $2,500 without the need for a formal budget adjustment. The overall allocation of $6,400 for the "other cost" category would not be affected by this transaction.

Focusing on the Budget's Purpose

A budget's purpose is to allocate funds to carry out the work programs. The budget should specify what these programs will be and what they intend to accomplish. The allocations or appropriations made by the budget should be to intervention programs, not to expenditure categories such as personal services or contractual services. However, for each intervention program, a breakdown of cost by major expenditure category should be provided. This shows what is needed to carry out a program. Increases or decreases in the allocations for these major expenditure categories can influence the performance of a program. For example, if a program requires three people but the allocation for personal services will only cover the cost of two people, then the effectiveness of the program will be jeopardized. Budget proposals, then, should show the relationships between various funding levels for intervention programs and their effect on the performance of these programs. Without this information, policy makers cannot make informed decisions about funding allocations and priorities.

Discussion Questions

1. What are the intervention activities that will make up our work programs for the current budget year?

2. What are the operating and administrative components of each of the intervention activities?

3. What will be the total cost of each of the operating and administrative components for the current budget year?

4. What will be the cost of managing the work of the collaborative for the current budget year?

5. What will be the sources of income to cover management of the collaborative and the costs of the interventions?

6. Who must approve the budget for the current year?

7. Who will administer the budget after it is adopted?

8. Will the budget itemize the work programs for the year?

9. Will the collaborative receive monthly reports on the status of the budget and the performance of the work programs?

Step 7 Monitoring and Evaluating

After collaboratives have adopted and implemented their strategy plans, they will need a system to monitor and evaluate the implementation, performance, and effectiveness of the interventions contained in these plans. This system will enable collaboratives to identify any problems with the execution of the interventions; note changes that may be needed in the interventions; and keep management and collaborative members informed about the performance and effectiveness of the interventions. It will also provide data to keep the public and funding bodies informed about the work of collaboratives and the performance of the intervention programs they have implemented.

Both the monitoring and evaluation elements of the system should focus on the plan. Otherwise, there is no value in developing the plan. Remember, the plan defines the goals and objectives, specifies the strategies and interventions that will be used to meet the objectives, assigns responsibility for implementing the strategies and interventions, establishes performance standards for the interventions, and specifies the procedures for connecting the target groups to the interventions. If a plan has any validity and if its contents are truly viewed as the policy decisions on actions to be taken to help children and their families, then monitoring and evaluation are needed to determine if the plan is being carried out and whether it is achieving the intended results. If the monitoring and evaluation aspects of the system do not focus on the various decisions contained in the plan, then clearly performance under the plan is not viewed as being of sufficient interest and concern to warrant attention. If this is the reality, then why spend the time,

energy, and money to develop a plan that is viewed as nothing more than a formality that can be placed on the shelf and forgotten!

This chapter is based on the assumption that the plans produced by collaboratives represent major policy decisions. Also, collaboratives want their plans to be implemented and want them to be effective. Finally, collaboratives want to know if their plans are being implemented in the manner specified and if they are achieving the results intended. Given these assumptions, the starting point for monitoring and evaluating must be the plan itself.

In this manual, monitoring and evaluating are viewed as a continuum of data collection and analysis to provide relevant information about the operations under a plan. *Monitoring*, as used in this manual, is *an activity that focuses primarily on issues that management should address in overseeing the implementation of the plan.* *Evaluating*, as used in this manual, addresses the same issues, as well as other related issues, and is *a means whereby a program or collaborative can be systematically assessed.* Each of these processes is discussed in this chapter.

Monitoring

The management of collaboratives will need a system for monitoring the execution of the strategy plan. This system should be designed to supply management with the necessary information to properly oversee the implementation, performance, and effectiveness of the strategies and interventions contained in the plan. To meet this need, the monitoring sys-

75

tem should address the following questions, among others:

1. *Are time schedules for implementing the plan being met?* As discussed in Chapter 7, when starting new programs, a timetable for putting them into operation should be established. This schedule should list the dates for beginning and completing the actions needed to make the programs operational, including hiring and training staff, drafting operational procedures, purchasing start-up supplies and equipment, renting office space, and negotiating the contracts (if any) for providing intervention services specified in the strategy plan. This schedule becomes an instrument for monitoring progress. If management determines that the time lines in the schedule are not appropriate, they can be revised. If management finds that delays in meeting time lines indicate a lack of effort by staff, it can take corrective action. Without a timetable for actions, however, there is no effective way to manage the timeliness of program implementation.

2. *Are the performance components for the interventions in place, and are they effective?* The performance components for interventions may include the following:

   a. *Contact procedures.* Children and their families from groups targeted for intervention services can be brought into the interventions by self-referrals, by agency referrals, and by outreach contacts. The plan should specify the contact procedure that will be used and a standard for measuring the success of the contact procedure. The monitoring system should determine if this contact procedure is in place and if the standard for success has been met. For example, a target group for an intervention service might consist of 200 unwed teenage mothers. The monitoring system might find that 20 members from this group entered the inter-

vention. If the performance standard called for 150 members to enter the intervention, then the information provided by the monitoring system shows that this standard was not met. The monitoring system should also identify the reasons why it was not met.

   b. *Intake system.* The management system for the interventions may call for a central intake system for consumers entering the intervention. In this case, the monitoring process should determine whether or not this intake system is in place and whether or not the procedures established for it are being followed.

   c. *A system for assessing consumers and developing intervention plans for them.* A performance standard for the interventions specified in the strategy plan may call for the children entering the interventions and their families to be assessed by a central unit. This standard may also call for the development of a custom-designed intervention plan that is based on the assessment and that is prepared for and with each child and his/her family. The monitoring system will determine if this performance standard is being met.

3. *Is progress being made in accomplishing the objectives?* The strategies are designed to accomplish specified objectives. Progress or lack of progress in accomplishing these objectives must be monitored. If the monitoring system finds that little or no progress is being made, then an analysis will be needed to determine the reasons. It may be that the required performance standards are not being met or the specified interventions are not being provided. Possibly, target group members are not following their intervention plans, or management of the intervention plans is falling short. Or, the interventions specified in the plans are found to be ineffective. Whatever the reasons, management will need to address them.

Progress or lack of progress in accomplishing objectives must be monitored.

determine if income projections are being met, and (2) to determine if program costs are staying within their allocation limits. Both these determinations are needed to help the collaborative avoid financial problems. In addition, the work programs specified in the budget must be monitored to ensure that they are being carried out accordingly, that performance standards are being met, and that objectives are being achieved.

5. *Are contract requirements being met?* A contract is of little value if its provisions are ignored. Not only can lack of compliance with contract provisions result in a waste of funds, but it can also result in consumers going without the intervention services called for in the contract. Contracts must be monitored to ensure compliance with their provisions and performance requirements. If a compliance default is found, management must act to correct this condition.

4. *Is the budget being followed?* The budget must be monitored for two reasons: (1) to

Table 19 illustrates a format for monitoring the timetable for implementing the plan and

TABLE 19		
Monitoring Start-up Schedules and Target Participation		
Activity	**Standard to Be Met**	**Was Standard Met?**

Start-up events
  Employ staff
  Train staff
  Adopt outreach system
  Adopt intake procedures
  Adopt assessment procedures
  Execute agreements with intervention agencies
  Adopt information system
  Begin entering target group members into interventions
	Date to be completed	*Date completed*

Target group and size of group
  Pregnant teenage girls:
  Teen mothers:
  Children of teen mothers less than 12 months old:
	Standard participation rate for target group members	*Participation rate for target group members*

for monitoring the participation of the members of the target group. A format for monitoring the performance standards for interventions is shown in Table 20. Table 21 is a means of monitoring the performance of the administrative components of an intervention plan and service integration issues (see page 80). Monitoring progress in achieving the outcomes is addressed in Table 22, and Table 23 illustrates a format for monitoring contract and budget compliance (see page 81). Although shown separately, the issues contained in Tables 19–23 are interrelated. Without this type of monitoring, the implementation of the strategy plan will not be managed and controlled. Instead, implementation will proceed without any oversight regarding accountability and responsibility for performance or results. If this happens, collaboratives will not be fulfilling their governing responsibilities. Furthermore, significant progress in helping children avoid or overcome barriers to successful adulthood is unlikely.

Evaluating

The preceding section describes the issues that the management of collaboratives should monitor in order to control the execution and performance of the strategy plans. In addition to a monitoring system, collaboratives will need an evaluation plan. This evaluation plan should be designed to address the information needs of funders, collaboratives, and members of the public.

1. *The funders:* Public and private organizations that provide funds to plan, implement, and manage the interventions will want to know if the interventions are accomplishing the objectives to which they are directed. For example, is an intervention to keep teenage mothers in school through to graduation achieving this result? These organizations will also want to know if the interventions are operating efficiently. For example, what is the annual cost per teenage mother of the intervention to keep the mother in school? How does the cost per mother compare with that for similar interventions in the community or in other communities?

2. *The collaborative:* Collaborative boards will want to be informed about the following:

   a. The performance and effectiveness of the interventions.

   b. The compliance of organizations with their contracts.

   c. Management's success in coordinating services.

   d. The compliance of expenditures with revenue collections in the budget.

   e. Changes needed in the design and/or management of the interventions.

   f. The proportion of target group members using the interventions and if this conforms to the performance standards established for the interventions.

   g. The value the members of the target group place on the interventions and their satisfaction with the administration and accessibility of the services.

   h. Community support for the efforts of the collaborative and the responsiveness of the community to the initiatives of the collaborative.

   i. The collaborative's success in keeping the public informed about the well-being of children and their families.

   j. The effectiveness of the collaborative as a decision-making body.

3. *The public:* The public will want to know whether or not the objectives established for the interventions are being achieved; for example, if the objective of reducing the school dropout rate is being achieved. The public will also want to know how much money is being spent for the interventions and whether or not the interventions are making a difference.

	TABLE 20
	Monitoring Performance Standards for Interventions

Performance Standard	Extent to Which Standard Is Being Met
Family Planning 1. All members of the target group will receive a health check and a family planning prescription. 2. Each pregnant member of the target group will receive a health screening and a prenatal plan to follow during the pregnancy. The plan will list the nutrition prescriptions, the prescriptions for controlling alcohol and drug use, and other appropriate prescriptions to ensure a healthy birth of the baby. 3. All members of the target group will fulfill the prescriptions for family planning and health care. 4. All pregnant members of the target group will fulfill the prescriptions for prenatal care.	
Remedial Education and Tutoring 1. All members of the target group who are behind in grade will be identified, and all will be assessed and placed into the appropriate remedial education and tutoring program. 2. All members of the target group who are school dropouts will be identified and either returned to school or entered into a GED program. 3. All members of the target group in tutoring or in remedial education will fulfill the attendance requirements and will complete the instructions. 4. All members of the target group who are behind in grade will, through tutoring and remedial education, advance to their proper grade within 12 months and will remain at the proper grade levels through graduation from high school.	
Day Care Support 1. All children of target mothers will be enrolled during school hours in a day care program that emphasizes early childhood development . 2. Each target mother will spend the specified number of hours per week at the day care center.	
Parenting Training 1. All target mothers will be enrolled in the parenting training program. 2. All target mothers will meet the attendance requirements of the program. 3. All target mothers will complete the parenting training program and demonstrate mastery of the skills presented in the training.	
Child Well-Being 1. All children of teenage mothers will receive immunization shots before the age of two years old. 2. All children of teenage mothers will receive regular health checks and health care. 3. All children of teenage mothers will receive cognitive development assistance during their first three years of life. 4. All children of teenage mothers will be enrolled in pre-K and kindergarten.	

TABLE 21	
Monitoring Administrative Performance and Service Integration Issues	
Administrative Performance Standard	**Extent to Which Standard Is Being Met**
Administrative Procedure 1. Each member of the target group will be visited at home not less than two times per month by an assigned case manager. 2. Each member will be contacted by a case manager by phone on appropriate dates to remind the member to follow the prescription and to attend appointments at the health clinic. Case managers will maintain compliance records on their respective charges. 3. All members of the target group will be identified, and all will be contacted by the outreach staff. 4. All members of the target group will be entered into the intervention services. 5. All members of the target group will enter the services through a central intake center, and all will be assessed and assisted in developing an intervention plan. 6. Case managers will submit a monthly report on their clients. The report will identify the number of clients assigned to them, the participation rate for these clients in the interventions, the compliance of the clients with the prescriptions, the performance of the agencies serving the clients, and the effectiveness of the interventions on the clients. **Service Integration** 1. Establish central intake and assessment system. 2. Establish consolidated information system. 3. Establish consolidated case management system. 4. Establish consolidated referral and follow-up system. 5. Establish system for coordinating complementary interventions. 6. Establish consolidated intervention budget. **Other**	

TABLE 22	
Monitoring Progress in Achieving Outcomes	
Outcome for Target Group	**Extent to Which Outcome Is Being Achieved**
1. All target group teenage mothers with children less than 12 months old will remain free of further births until they graduate from high school or earn a GED and reach the age of 20.	
2. All target group pregnant teenage girls will remain free of further pregnancies and births until they graduate from high school or earn a GED and reach the age of 20.	
3. Reduce the repeat pregnancy rate in the target 15–19 year-old age group from 51 per 1,000 to 21 per 1,000 within five years.	
4. All children of teenage mothers will be free of correctable disabilities and preventable diseases.	
5. All children of teenage mothers will not be retained in grade beginning in the first grade and will read at grade level.	
6. All children of teenage mothers will be free of abuse and neglect.	

TABLE 23		
Monitoring Contract and Budget Compliance		
Activity	**Standard to Be Met**	**Extent to Which Outcome Objective Is Being Achieved**
Contracts	**Contract Requirements**	**Was Contract Requirement Met?**
1. Prenatal care	a.	
	b.	
	c.	
2. Family planning services	a.	
	b.	
	c.	
3. Outreach, intake, and assessment services	a.	
	b.	
	c.	
Budget	**Budget Requirement**	**Budget Compliance**
1. Revenues estimates		
2. Appropriations by intervention		
3. Appropriations for management		
4. Appropriations by major expenditure code		
5. Other		

Designing an Evaluation Plan

To develop a useful evaluation plan, collaboratives must determine what they want to evaluate, how the evaluation will be carried out, and the purposes of the evaluation. These and related matters are addressed in the guidebook entitled *Pathways for Assessing Change* (September 1996), prepared for the Georgia Community Partnership Initiative by Metis Associates, Inc. Copies of this guidebook can be obtained from the Georgia Policy Council for Children and Families and from The Family Connection.

This guidebook defines *evaluation* as "a systematic and organized way to assess a program or collaborative." It also describes what evaluation does and how to conduct it.

A comprehensive evaluation examines the goals of a program, whether and how objectives are being met, and the outcomes associated with programs or system components. It can be conducted using qualitative methods (e.g., observations, interviews, surveys) and/or quantitative methods (e.g., statistical analysis of data). Evaluation is an integral part of the ongoing process of planning, implementation, and improvement—it yields information needed by program staff and management, policy makers and funders, as well as the community at large.

Evaluation is a systematic and organized way to assess a program or collaborative.

The guidebook points out that evaluation can be performed on behalf of the collaborative by an outside consultant or by the self-evaluation of those who design and operate the program. The resource is intended to serve as a guide for self-evaluation, and the resulting information "can be used to—

- monitor program implementation;
- determine if a program, activity, service, or strategy is meeting its goals and objectives;
- identify areas of unmet or emerging needs;
- make changes needed to improve quality of programs or strategies;
- provide information to staff that will improve job satisfaction and performance;
- support requests for public or private funding; and
- provide information that will increase awareness of or support for the program, activity or strategy."

A self-evaluation format has also been developed for Family Connection communities. Copies of this format can be obtained from the offices of The Family Connection.[1]

---

1. The Family Connection, 100 Peachtree Street NW, Suite 500, Atlanta, GA 30303. Phone (404) 527-7394.

Discussion Questions

1. What information does the collaborative need in order to manage effectively the implementation and administration of the strategies and interventions?

2. What information do the members of the collaborative need to fulfill their governing responsibilities?

3. What information do the agencies, organizations, and staff need to help them perform their work on behalf of the collaborative?

4. What information is needed to keep the funders and public informed about the work of the collaborative?

5. Who will perform the evaluation? Will it be a self-evaluation, or will the evaluation be performed by an outside evaluator?

6. How timely should the information be that is provided by the evaluation?

7. How will the information obtained through the evaluation be used?

8. Who will receive the results of the evaluation?

10 Summing Up

Systematic, comprehensive, and informed planning in a collaborative setting is hard work. It requires patience, data collection, analytical thinking, and creative and innovative strategy development. Above all, it requires the collaboration of all the people, agencies, organizations, and institutions whose actions (or inactions) can affect both the ability of children in the community to achieve successful adulthood and the ability of parents to provide the protective support children need to develop successfully. This collaboration is essential for reaching agreement on goals for children. It is needed to gain the support and assistance from agencies in measuring baseline conditions for these goals, which in turn will help in developing information about the risk factors that affect the baseline conditions.

Planning in a collaborative setting is hard work.

Most significantly, collaboration is the critical ingredient in designing and implementing integrated, complementary, and coordinated intervention systems to reduce the numbers of children who experience success inhibiters.

Developing a Work Plan

Collaboratives will find that their planning work will proceed more quickly and smoothly if they first develop an outline. To be useful, this outline should identify each of the tasks that must be completed. This outline will help the collaborative to—

1. focus the planning work;
2. identify all of the issues that the plan should address; and
3. provide a basis for establishing a schedule for completing the plan.

Examples of a plan preparation work outline and plan summary are presented in Appendix B.

Staffing the Planning Effort

To accomplish the work specified in the outline requires a staff. This staff support can be obtained in several ways:

1. If it has the legal power to do so, the collaborative can employ staff.
2. Staff can be loaned to the organization by public and private agencies in the community. For example, a staff person could be assigned from such organizations as the school system, health department, munici-

pal or county governments, and United Way.

3. Staff can be obtained by contracting with a consultant.

A director should be designated to be in charge of the staff and in charge of the planning effort. This director must have the authority and responsibility for managing the work and developing proposed strategies for the plan. The director should also develop time lines for completing each of the work tasks and should monitor compliance with these time lines.

Obtaining Technical Assistance

Collaboratives may need technical assistance when developing their plans. They may need help to develop their goals, identify their data needs, develop their strategies, and design their funding plans and information systems. This help can be obtained from consultants, from local colleges, from the state university system, and/or from state agencies that are a part of The Family Connection initiative or the Georgia Policy Council on Children and Families initiative. In Georgia, for example, technical assistance is available from and through Family Connection facilitators, from support staff in state agencies, and from consultants working with The Family Connection and the Georgia Policy Council on Children and Families. This assistance is available to Family Connection collaboratives and to Community Partnership collaboratives.

Making a Difference

This manual has presented a process for developing plans to help children become successful adults. Data from many sources indi-

cate that the need for this help is urgent: rates for delinquency, unwed teenage parenthood, school dropouts, and youth unemployment and inactivity continue to be unacceptable. The data also show that children who are experiencing these conditions are often at high risk for not achieving successful adulthoods.

There is much rhetoric about such children and their families. The conditions of these children are reported in the media, discussed in Congress, and talked about at numerous conferences on youth. Despite the rhetoric, however, helping children avoid or overcome these conditions has yet to become a high-priority public policy issue. Perhaps the reason for this is that children cannot vote. However, perhaps the more plausible explanation is that the relationship between unsuccessful childhoods and unsuccessful adulthoods is not recognized, understood, and acted on. The failure to recognize that this can be a detrimental relationship is creating both high social costs and high economic costs. The social costs are measured in terms of crime, a less productive workforce, wasted lives, poverty, drug and alcohol abuse, delinquency, and abuse and neglect. Economic costs reflect these same conditions in terms of prisons, public assistance, and publicly financed health care.

Social costs affect the quality of life of communities; economic costs affect the public's pocketbooks. Both types of cost need attention. If these costs are to be controlled, the communities, the states, and the nation cannot continue to be indifferent to their effect on children. Designing effective actions to address the conditions of children requires intelligent and skillful planning. In addition, it requires committed public will and committed public funding to implement the plans produced by these efforts.

Collaboratives must use their power and influence to obtain the policies and funding to develop and execute effective plans. To do this, collaboratives will need governing boards whose members have power and influence in the community. Collaboratives will also need boards whose members and staffs can develop responsive plans to gain the public's attention and support. Finally, these boards will need to be committed to helping all children experience successful childhoods and achieve successful adulthoods.

Can collaboratives make a difference in the outcomes that children experience? Indeed they can. The key to their success lies in the quality, commitment, and ability of their governing boards. It will also depend on the effectiveness of their boards in gaining public support and participation in their efforts to make a difference.

Glossary

(Terms are defined according to their usage in this manual.)

Baseline Condition: Quantified measurement of the extent to which the real world does not conform to the ideal condition specified in the goal.

Budget: The adopted plan for an operating year that specifies the work programs, the costs of this work, the revenue sources that will be used to pay these costs, and the appropriation that will be made from these revenues to cover these costs.

Budgeting: The process by which the annual work programs are developed, the cost of the work is calculated, and the means of financing this cost are identified.

Collaborative: An organization whose members collectively agree and commit themselves to the following:

• To serve as advocates and activists for children.

• To adopt a common vision for successful outcomes for children.

• To adopt and agree on common goals for children.

• To adopt and agree on objectives for achieving these goals.

• To adopt and agree on strategies for achieving these objectives.

• To adopt and agree on annual work programs and budgets to implement the strategies.

• To ensure that participating agencies and institutions in the collaborative agree to carry out the components of the strategies assigned to them.

• To ensure that participating agencies and institutions in the collaborative agree to allocate or redirect funds to pay the costs of implementing the strategies assigned to them.

• To ensure that members of the collaborative are individually and collectively responsible for the performance and effectiveness of the strategies.

• To ensure that participating agencies and institutions coordinate interventions to serve children and their families.

• To minimize and eliminate duplication of efforts on the part of the collaborative members.

• To eliminate competition among agencies and institutions for funds and recognition.

• To ensure that participating agencies and institutions objectively, candidly, and completely report results of their interventions to help children and their families.

Evaluating: A means whereby a program or collaborative can be systematically assessed.

Goal: Specification of the ideal condition that must exist if a vision is to be achieved. A standard that can be used to compare the real world with the ideal world.

Intervention: A systematic attempt to achieve an objective by reducing or eliminating the risk factors that make children vulnerable to the success inhibiters and/or by creating protective factors that can keep them from becoming vulnerable to the success inhibiters.

Monitoring: An activity that focuses primarily on issues that management should address in overseeing the implementation of a plan.

Objective: A targeted outcome to be achieved in the baseline condition within a specified time.

Plan: The decisions made through the planning process about the goals that will be pursued and the means that will be used to accomplish these goals.

Planning: A systematic process whereby plans are developed to accomplish specified goals and objectives.

Protective Factor: Condition in the lives of children that provides them with the motivation and capacity to avoid or overcome a success inhibiter.

Risk Factors: Conditions in the lives of children that deny them the motivation and capacity to avoid or overcome the success inhibiters that can be barriers to their achieving successful adulthood.

Strategy: An intervention or a combination of complementary and coordinated interventions directed toward achieving an objective.

Success Inhibiter: Condition experienced by children that can be a barrier to the development of the values, skills, motivations, capacities, and personal relationships they need to become successful adults.

Vision: A perfect world condition that is to be achieved in the future through the work of the collaborative. It is a destination to be reached, a dream to be pursued.

TASK PLAN FOR COLLABORATIVES

Task to Be Completed	Responsible Committee/Individual	Date to Be Completed
Create a governing collaborative		
1. Define mission of the collaborative		
2. Determine type of collaborative		
a. A meet-and-confer body		
b. A private, nonprofit corporation		
c. A quasi-governmental commission		
3. Specify the legal powers of the collaborative		
4. Determine composition of the collaborative's governing body		
a. Size of the governing body		
b. Qualifications to be considered for membership		
i. Elected officials from municipal and county governments		
ii. Chief administrative officers of municipal and county governments		
iii. Business community representatives		
iv. Director of the Department of Family and Children Services		
v. Director of the health department		
vi. Executive from the Department of Juvenile Justice		
vii. Superintendent of schools		
viii. Chairman of the school board		
ix. Civic club board members		
x. Private, nonprofit social services board members		
xi. Citizens concerned about children and families		
xii. Ministerial association representatives		
xiii. Representatives from target populations		
xiv. Others		
c. How members will be appointed		
d. Terms of office		
5. Adopt a vision for the collaborative whereby—		
a. Progress in achieving it can be measured		
b. Desired outcomes for children and their families are specified		
6. Adopt procedures to inform the community about the well-being of children and families		

TASK PLAN FOR COLLABORATIVES

Task to Be Completed	Responsible Committee/Individual	Date to Be Completed

Develop a comprehensive plan (see Appendix B)
1. Adopt goals
2. Determine baseline conditions
3. Identify risk factors and target groups
4. Establish objectives
5. Design strategies and interventions
   a. Adopt performance standards and specifications
   b. Designate responsible agencies
6. Design implementation plan, establishing—
   a. Means of holding responsible agencies accountable
   b. Means of coordinating interventions
   c. System for monitoring the implementation and performance of the interventions
7. Adopt a budget for implementing the plan
8. Design an evaluation plan, addressing—
   a. What will be evaluated?
   b. Who will do the evaluating?
   c. How will the evaluation be used?
   d. How will the cost of the evaluation be funded?
 	
Develop a plan for making policy and system changes, creating—
1. Integrated outreach and referral procedures
2. A centralized intake and assessment system
3. An integrated information system
4. A system for coordinating referrals for interventions and follow up
5. A coordinated and/or integrated case management system
6. A co-location system for intervention services
7. A consolidated budget and funding pool for interventions
8. A cross-agency training system		

PLAN PREPARATION WORK OUTLINE

I. Adopt goals
    A. Set goals for children
    B. Set goals for adolescents

II. Measure baseline conditions
    A. Measure extent to which each of the goals is being met
    B. Break down measurements as appropriate by age, gender, race

III. Identify risk factors
    A. Identify appropriate risk factors for the baseline conditions:
        1. Pre-birth
        2. Individual
        3. Family
        4. Neighborhood
        5. Economic
        6. Service delivery
        7. Success inhibiters:
            a. Low birthweight
            b. Abuse and neglect
            c. Unwed teenage motherhood
            d. School failure
            e. Criminal delinquency
            f. Other

IV. Adopt objectives
    A. Improve baseline rates and numbers by—
        1. Relating objectives to baseline conditions for success inhibiters for—
            a. Children experiencing success inhibiters
            b. Children vulnerable to success inhibiters
        2. Relating objectives to baseline conditions for risk factors

V. Design the strategies and interventions
    A. Accomplish the objectives by identifying—
        1. Success inhibiters to be addressed
        2. Objectives to be addressed
        3. Risk factors to be addressed
        4. Geographic area the interventions will target
        5. Risk groups to be targeted
        6. Categories of children to be served:
            a. Those experiencing success inhibiters
            b. Those vulnerable to success inhibiters
        7. Protective factors to be strengthened

VI. Design performance standards and specifications for the strategies and interventions

PLAN PREPARATION WORK OUTLINE

VII. Design administrative procedures, including—

    A. Outreach and referral procedures to bring target group members into the interventions

    B. Intake procedures

    C. Procedures to assess, as appropriate to individual target group members—

        1. Success inhibiters to be prevented or mitigated

        2. Risk factors to be addressed

        3. Protective factors to be strengthened

    D. Specifications for intervention plans, as appropriate to individual target group members—

        1. Objectives to be achieved

        2. Interventions to be used and performance standards to be met

        3. Procedures for managing and monitoring the intervention plans

VIII. Design and execute the strategy plan

    A. Design a management system

    B. Adopt procedures for providing the intervention services—

        1. Arrange for existing agencies to provide the services—

            a. By contract

            b. By memorandum of understanding

            c. By memorandum of agreement

        2. Create a new intervention agency

        3. Arrange for the collaborative to provide the intervention

    C. Coordinate the interventions

    D. Monitor the intervention plan implementation, determining if—

        1. The schedule for implementing the plan is being met

        2. The performance standards specified are being met

        3. The budget plan is being followed

        4. The contract requirements or agreements are being met

        5. The interventions are achieving the desired results

IX. Adopt a budget for the intervention plan

PLAN SUMMARY							
Goal:							
Baseline Conditions	Risk Factors	Target Group	Objectives	Strategies/ Interventions	Performance Standards	Responsible Agencies	Budget Allocation

GEORGIA'S BENCHMARKS FOR CHILDREN AND FAMILIES

Healthy Children

- Increase the percentage of babies born healthy (weighing 5.5 pounds or more, born to mothers who received prenatal care the first trimester, and born to mothers who did not smoke or drink alcohol during pregnancy).
- Increase the percentage of children appropriately immunized by the age of two.
- Reduce the pregnancy rate among school-age girls.
- Reduce the percentage of children who have untreated vision, hearing, or health problems at school entry.
- Reduce the teenage homicide rate.
- Increase the percentage of youths who do not use alcohol, tobacco, or illegal drugs.

Children Ready for School

- Increase the percentage of low-income students in Head Start or prekindergarten programs.
- Increase the percentage of kindergarten students who attended preschool or child care programs.
- Increase the percentage of students passing the Georgia Kindergarten Assessment Program.
- Reduce the percentage of students who are two or more years overage in the third grade.

Children Succeeding in School

- Reduce the percentage of students who are absent ten or more days from school annually.
- Increase the percentage of students performing above state standards on curriculum-based tests at the fifth and eleventh grades.
- Increase the percentage of students scoring above the national median on normed achievement tests at the eighth grade.
- Increase the percentage of students who graduate from high school on time.
- Increase parental involvement.

Strong Families

- Increase the percentage of stable new families (with the first birth to a mother who has completed high school and is age 20 or older, and with the father's name recorded on the birth certificate).
- Reduce the percentage of teenage mothers who have a second or higher-order birth before the age of 20.
- Reduce the incidence of confirmed child abuse or neglect.
- Increase the percentage of children in foster care who are placed in a permanent home.
- Reduce the percentage of youths arrested.

Self-Sufficient Families

- Reduce the percentage of children living in poverty.
- Reduce the percentage of female-headed families living in poverty.
- Increase the percentage of welfare recipients leaving public assistance because of employment or higher incomes.
- Increase the rate of growth in employment.
- Reduce the unemployment rate.
- Increase affordable, accessible, quality child care.

Note: Reprinted from *Aiming for Results: A Guide to Georgia's Benchmarks for Children and Families* (Atlanta: Georgia Policy Council for Children and Families, 1996).

BUDGET PLAN
Budget Year
Name of Collaborative

1. BUDGET ALLOCATIONS BY SOURCES OF FUNDS

Budget Category	State Grant $	Local In-Kind $	Cash Match $	Source of Funds				
				Source $	Source $	Source $	Source $	Source $
Interventions								
1.								
2.								
3.								
4.								
Subtotal								
Administrative Components								
1.								
2.								
3.								
4.								
Subtotal								
Management								
1.								
2.								
3.								
4.								
Subtotal								
TOTAL								

BUDGET PLAN
Budget Year
Name of Collaborative

2. ALLOCATION SUMMARY

Activity	Allocation
Interventions	
1.	
2.	
3.	
4.	
5.	
Subtotal	
Administrative Components	
1.	
2.	
3.	
4.	
5.	
Subtotal	
Collaborative Management	
1.	
2.	
3.	
4.	
5.	
Subtotal	
TOTAL	

BUDGET PLAN
Budget Year
Name of Collaborative

3. SOURCE SUMMARY

Source	Amount/Value	Purpose
Local Cash Contributions[1]		
1.		
2.		
3.		
4.		
5.		
TOTAL		
In-Kind Contribution Sources[2]		
1.		
2.		
3.		
4.		
5.		
TOTAL		

[1] *Local cash:* This is cash contributed by local government, individuals, and/or private or public groups within the community. These funds may be restricted to certain costs or may be unrestricted and can be applied to any costs. If restricted, list the costs to which these funds must be applied. Note if unrestricted.

[2] *In-Kind contributions:* These contributions can be in the form of personnel, services, equipment, or other services that without the contribution would be a cost to the collaborative. The in-kind contributions may be earmarked for specified activities of the collaborative or may be unrestricted. If restricted, list the specified activities.

BUDGET PLAN
Budget Year
Name of Collaborative

4. ALLOCATIONS OF GRANT FUNDS

Amount of Grant: $ _____

Budget Categories[3]	Amount Allocated	Name of Intervention or Activity and Amount Allocated				
1. Personal services						
2. Regular operating						
3. Travel						
4. Equipment						
5. Real estate rentals						
6. Per diem fees and contracts						
7. Telecommunications						
8. Utilities						
9. Other (specify)						
TOTAL						

[3] See the state's Chart of Accounts that identifies the items of cost under each of the budget categories.

BUDGET PLAN
Budget Year
Name of Collaborative

5. BUDGET ALLOCATIONS BY BUDGET CATEGORIES

Activity	Categories							
	Personal Services	Regular Operating	Travel	Equipment	Real Estate Rentals	Per Diem Fees and Contracts	Telecommu- nications	Utilities	Other	Total
Interventions								
1.								
2.								
3.								
4.								
Subtotal								
Administrative Components								
1.								
2.								
3.								
4.								
Subtotal								
Collaborative Management								
1.								
2.								
3.								
4.								
Subtotal								
TOTAL								

CHECKLIST FOR CREATING A LEGALLY EMPOWERED GOVERNING STRUCTURE FOR A COLLABORATIVE

	Yes/No

1. The governing body has been created—
   a. by a charter creating a private, nonprofit corporation. _____
   b. by legislation authorizing the creation of a governing body. _____

2. The Governing Board has obtained 501 (c) 3 clearance from the Internal Revenue Service for the collaborative. _____

3. The Governing Board has the following legal powers specifically granted by the charter of incorporation or by the legislation authorizing the governing board:
   a. To have a seal and alter the same at its pleasure. _____
   b. To acquire, hold, and dispose of in its own name by purchase, gift, lease, or exchange, on such terms and conditions and in such manner and by such instrument as it may deem proper, real and personal property of every kind, character, and description, but shall not have the power to acquire any real or personal property by condemnation or eminent domain. _____
   c. To procure insurance against any loss in connection with its property and other assets of the community partnership. _____
   d. To make contracts and to execute all instruments necessary or convenient in connection therewith. _____
   e. To adopt, alter, or repeal its own bylaws, rules, and regulations governing the manner in which its business may be transacted and in which the power granted to it may be enjoyed, as the governing body may deem necessary or expedient in facilitating its business. _____
   f. To receive, accept, and utilize gifts, grants, donations, or contributions of money, property, facilities, or services, with or without consideration, from any person, firm, corporation, foundation, or other entity or from this state or any agency, instrumentality, or political subdivision thereof or from the United States or any agency or instrumentality thereof. _____
   g. To select, appoint, and employ professional, administrative, clerical, or other personnel and to contract for professional or other services and to allow suitable compensation for such personnel and services. _____
   h. To do all things necessary or convenient to carry out the powers and purposes of the governing body. _____

4. Members and organization:
   a. Members are appointed for specific terms of office as specified in the charter or legislation creating the governing board. _____
   b. Method of appointing members is specified in the charter or legislation creating the governing board. _____
   c. The legislation or charter specifies who the appointing authorities will be for making appointments to the governing board. _____
   d. The legislation or charter specifies the number of members the governing board will have. _____
   e. The legislation or charter specifies the officers the governing board will have and their terms of office. _____
   f. The legislation or charter specifies the minimum frequency with which the governing board will meet. _____
   g. The legislation or charter specifies the quorum for meetings of the governing board. _____

CHECKLIST FOR CREATING A LEGALLY EMPOWERED GOVERNING STRUCTURE FOR A COLLABORATIVE

	Yes/No
h. The membership on the board includes representatives from the following groups:	
i. Local elected officials from county and/or municipal government.	
ii. Municipal and/or county managers.	_____
iii. Elected members of the school board.	_____
iv. Superintendent of Schools.	_____
v. Persons from the business community.	_____
vi. Heads of departments from the Department of Human Resources.	_____
vii. Management head from the Department of Children and Youth Services.	_____
viii. Representative from the Department of Education.	_____
ix. Representatives from the boards of civic organizations.	_____
x. Representatives from private, nonprofit social service providers.	_____
xi. Advocates for children and families from the community.	_____
xii. Representatives from the target populations.	_____
xiii. Representatives from religious organizations.	_____
xiv. Representatives from the local legislative delegation.	_____
xv. Other.	_____

5. Bylaws:
    a. Specify terms of office for members as specified in the charter or legislation.
    b. Specify that the member will be appointed in the manner specified in the charter or legislation.
    c. Specify the manner of selecting officers and their terms of office consistent with the requirement of the charter or legislation, and specify their duties.
    d. Specify the duties and responsibilities of the executive director or coordinator.
    e. Specify meeting schedule for the board consistent with the charter or legislation.
    f. Require financial audits and financial reporting.
    g. Specify compensation or reimbursement of the members of the governing board.

6. Community participation and public awareness:
    a. Annual or regular reports are made to the community on the condition of children and families in the community.
    b. Representatives from stakeholder groups and the public who are not members of the governing board serve on committees created by the governing board.
    c. Ex officio nonvoting members are appointed to the board.
    d. Meetings of the governing board are regularly reported in the media.

7. Training:
    a. Board organizes and conducts interagency training programs on interventions, intervention procedures, and other matters relating to the development and implementation of the plan.
    b. Board members and staff receive training on their responsibilities.
    c. Board holds annual retreats to review performance of interventions and to consider changes in the plan.

CHECKLIST FOR CREATING A LEGALLY EMPOWERED GOVERNING STRUCTURE FOR A COLLABORATIVE

	Yes/No
8. Functions of the collaborative's governing board:	
a. Adopts goals.	_____
b. Adopts strategy plans.	_____
c. Adopts budget.	_____
d. Authorizes contracts.	_____
e. Appoints executive director or coordinator.	_____
f. Establishes policy for the operation of the collaborative.	_____
g. Reviews performance of contracts and acts to achieve compliance.	_____
h. Reviews results being achieved through the interventions and acts to change or strengthen interventions that are found to be ineffective.	_____
i. Makes presentations about the work of the collaborative to civic organizations and other groups in the community.	_____
j. Appears before the governing bodies of the county and municipalities to advocate for children.	_____